HEROES
NEED NOT
APPLY

How to Build a
Patient-Accountable
Culture Without
Putting More
on Your Plate

Brian D. Wong, MD, MPH

SECOND RIVER
HEALTHCARE

HEROES NEED NOT APPLY:
How to Build a Patient-Accountable Culture
Without Putting More on Your Plate

Second River Healthcare
A Healthcare Leadership Publishing Company
26 Shawnee Way, Suite C
Bozeman, MT 59715
Phone (406) 586-8775 | FAX (406) 586-5672

Editors: Amy Lukens and Tiffany L. Young
Cover Design: Lan Weisberger – Design Solutions
Typesetting/Composition: Neuhaus/Tyrrell Graphic Design
Editing Style: The Chicago Manual of Style – Sixteenth Edition

Wong, Brian D.
HEROES NEED NOT APPLY: How to Build a Patient-Accountable Culture Without Putting More on Your Plate / Brian D. Wong, MD, MPH

ISBN-13: 978-1-936406-23-4 (hardcover)
ISBN-13: 978-1-936406-24-1 (softcover)
ISBN-13: 978-1-936406-25-8 (e-Book)

1. Physician Leadership   2. Healthcare Culture   3. Patient Safety

Library of Congress Control Number: 2013937587

First Printing   September 2013

Second River Healthcare books are available at special quantity discounts. Please call for information at: (406) 586-8775 or order from the website:
www.SecondRiverHealthcare.com or **www.HeroesNeedNotApply.com**

TABLE OF CONTENTS

PRAISE FOR HEROES NEED NOT APPLY

As a former health system chief executive who has experienced failure and the awful tragedy that came with it, I appreciate what Dr. Wong's book, *Heroes Need Not Apply*, has to say about the critical nature of being human as a leader. So often we use our position or our profession as a barrier to the intimacy required to engage in deep dialogue and operate as a true team on behalf of the patient. Individual expertise, like any other strength, when driven to excess becomes a weakness. Brian illustrates this through his characters' journey of courage and renewal, as they open themselves to the realization that a patient's death lay within the gaps created by hierarchy, blame, and isolation. Being fully present, listening without judgment, living in service to others, and respect are critical elements in a just, safe, and patient-oriented culture. While Dr. Wong's story and his characters are fictional, he speaks the truth of what we must become as leaders in healthcare.

Jeff Selberg
EVP and Chief Operating Officer
Institute for Healthcare Improvement

As parents, we experienced the devastating effects of wrongful death when we lost our son to a preventable medical error. Dr. Wong's book offers profound insight as to how these events continue to occur with such frequency, and the prescription healthcare leaders can use to put an end to this ongoing dilemma. *Heroes Need Not Apply* helps patients, family members, and healthcare professionals understand how to prevent patient harm and wrongful death. While this book's intent is to guide healthcare leaders, physicians, and nurses in the creation of safer hospitals, we hope every patient has the opportunity to read it in order to gain the awareness needed to help truly prevent "preventable errors" in the future.

David and Leta Goldberg
Parents of Alex J. Goldberg
(April 29, 1984 – June 16, 2011)

Brian Wong, MD, vividly describes the cultural challenges present in many hospitals and links the associated issues to the reality of the experience of patients. In this industry information is abundant, science is increasingly precise, and the best outcomes border on the miraculous. Wong reveals how all of these can go for naught when a culture of inequity, fear, and hierarchy result in insufficient communication and inadequate collaboration.

Unfortunately, these situations occur daily in hospitals all over the country. Fortunately there are also hundreds of hospitals that have confronted these destructive cultural realities. These hospitals have created cultures that are just, fair, and open. The results of these healthy positive cultures are remarkable improvements in quality, patient experience, safety, and employee morale.

There are many critical players in hospitals and healthcare systems that are needed to make the care truly safe, equitable, effective, and affordable. We need clinical teams with skilled nurses, pharmacists, technicians, and physicians. We also need deeply capable business leaders who understand operations, finance, and human resources. But the role of the physician stands out because we have a disproportionate impact on the healthcare system that our patients experience. With our disproportionate impact must come disproportionate accountability.

Wong points out many of the trials and challenges physicians face in trying to develop and run a successful practice. These challenges and barriers must be addressed to preserve and enhance the professional quality of physicians' careers. But as the career becomes vibrant and satisfying professionally, we must then ask physicians to become more fully accountable for the healthcare system that our patients need, want, and deserve.

Our patients encounter the healthcare system physically, socially, psychologically, and financially. As physicians we need to understand this and respond to the various challenges that patients experience in their healthcare journey. Physicians need to embrace the roles of healer, leader, and partner.

Physician as *Healer* brings excellent clinical skills and knowledge to the care of patients. But she also is aware of the fear and uncertainty in patients and families who have to experience healthcare and our interventions and institutions. Physician as *Healer* is an attitude, a commitment, and a style.

Physician as *Leader* recognizes the multiple ways in which patients encounter and experience the healthcare system. Physicians choose to "opt in" in the areas of healthcare that are traditionally beyond the bounds of their responsibility as clinician whether the issue be quality, access, safety, equity, or affordability. Physician as *Leader* accepts a broad level of responsibility for the challenges and realities of our patients. This requires an expanded view of accountability and can require investment of time and energy. If physicians elect to "opt out" of major non-clinical issues, then the patient loses an important voice and advocate.

Physician as *Partner* fully accepts that not only is excellent care a team effort, but that physicians can greatly impact career satisfaction of our nurses, pharmacists, technicians, and assistants. Physician as *Partner* is a compassionate team member and leader, but is also unwavering in setting expectations for the highest quality experience for our patients.

Brian Wong has presented so clearly and compellingly the role of the physician in the issues our patients are facing in healthcare today. He has also clarified that the career challenges for many doctors are real and some are daunting. For physicians to be fully responsive, responsible, and accountable leaders on behalf of our patients there must first be the improvements, interventions, and support to ensure that the professional career experience is preserved and enhanced. The responsibility of physicians is to use this excellent professional career platform to support and care for our patients in all of their experiences in healthcare by embracing the roles of *Healer, Leader*, and *Partner*.

Jack Cochran, MD
Executive Director
The Permanente Federation, LLC

As a physician executive who has spent most of my research career looking at what makes physicians different than others as to how we handle stress, change, and transformation, I appreciate how Dr. Wong's book, *Heroes Need Not Apply*, breaks new ground as a field manual for what WE can all do on the front lines to be leaders as opposed to "reactors" of healthcare transformation. Dr. Wong's innovative approach of storytelling to highlight the changes needed in how we perform on a day-to-day basis is a welcome alternative to the "self-help" books that, while accurate and helpful, do not have the life-changing effects that one read of this book may attain. Many of the precepts in this well-written book will be known to readers prior to opening the first page—teamwork, coordination of care, patient-centricity—but there is a "stickiness" to the way those pathways to future success are presented in this easily readable, hard-to-put-down book.

The staff of Angels of Seattle Hospital (names have been changed to protect all of us) work hard, want to do the right thing, and are convinced that the way they have been operating is in the best interests of patients. Sound familiar? Without preaching or professing, Dr. Wong puts us in the shoes of the doctors, nurses, administrators, and patients undergoing a series of well-meaning but significant breakdowns while trying to do the right thing for patients, themselves, and their colleagues. Culture change is a popular term nowadays, but it starts with "looking in the mirror" and making sure that wherever you fit in the healthcare delivery continuum, your mindset is ready for the reengineering that will undoubtedly occur at your hospital, health system, or practice. As Dr. Jack Martin, one of the protagonists in the book, put it, "Every good team needs a coach," and this field manual for an optimistic future in healthcare will serve as your virtual mentor during the whitewater of change that is inevitable during the next few years.

So what about a future that includes "treating each other with respect, being a team player, listening without judgment, and creating a place where everyone feels safe to contribute…"? That future is attainable, not only in this fictional health system in Washington State, but starting tomorrow after you read, and your colleagues read *Heroes Need Not Apply*. So, if you think that you will need to be a different doctor, nurse, health professional, or administrator to be successful five years from now, read this book. If you don't think anything will alter in healthcare and that you don't need any help "changing your DNA," then buy the book anyway and give it to a friend who wants to succeed and be happy in the new healthcare future.

Stephen K. Klasko, MD, MBA
President
Thomas Jefferson University
President and CEO
Thomas Jefferson University Health System

Dr. Wong's book is a profound story that shines an accurate light on the reality of what happens in the clinical area when anyone on the team shows up with "less than their best." As an experienced nurse, executive, and patient engagement specialist, I believe this book will help save lives, improve quality, and recommit healthcare providers and patients to new levels of trust.

Sue Collier, MSN, RN, FABC
Performance Improvement Specialist
Patient-Family Engagement
North Carolina Quality Center – North Carolina Hospital Association

Heroes Need Not Apply is an enlightening allegory of how preventable medical errors occur and what we can do about it. What makes the book so compelling is that Brian Wong has the credibility of an accomplished physician, the ear of a skilled storyteller, and the insights of an experienced consultant.

Dr. Wong illustrates the issue, one of the most important and seemingly intractable in modern medicine, through the account of a routine operation performed by an expert surgeon assisted by a highly capable staff. Following the same protocols had regularly produced successful outcomes—but not this time.

In an engaging and easy-to-read style, Dr. Wong explores the challenges and fears of everyone involved—physicians, nurses, administrators, and, of course, the patient and her family—from the series of events that led to the mistake to the investigation of how to prevent it from happening again.

Dr. Wong draws the reader into the world of the hospital and an understanding of the cultural barriers that contribute so much to preventable medical errors. After diagnosing the root cause, he then provides the prescription for effective change. *Heroes Need Not Apply* is a vitally important book for trustees, administrators, and clinicians who want to build a safer, more patient-centered culture but are unsure how to make it happen.

Gordon R. Clark
President and CEO
iProtean

This book strongly brings out your empathy and compassion for those who are on the opposite sides (patient, provider) of medical care. By focusing on the everyday struggles and the unhealthy work environments which exist, it gives the catalyst to continue to want to help heal the existing medical care system. It exposes those significant barriers, which are dangerous and counterproductive to healing (for both patient and care providers). It gives us hope that there is a better way to connect to our healing spirit and the reason why we entered the medical profession. Regaining trust, which comes from patient-focused care provided by healthy medical care teams, can again be the reality.

Randall Levin, MD, FACEP
Director for Physician Education
Medical Technology Management Institute
(A Continuing Education Division of Herzing University)
ACEP Wellness Section Newsletter Editor

Dr. Brian Wong personifies the rare triple threat—master physician, master executive, and master healthcare mentor/coach. Through training and experience, he has come to understand how the disparate hospital organisms (administration, board, and medical, nursing, and professional staff) can come together and realize safe, timely, efficient, effective, and equitable patient-centered care. His genius allows him to teach and coach that realization. In *Heroes Need Not Apply*, very real characters in a very real circumstance bring his message to life. On its own, it is a good read; however, I envision that his well-crafted story will prove to be an important collective read for the ascendant, enlightened hospital, serve as a fulcrum for dialogue among administration, board, and medical, nursing, and professional staff and enable immediate, necessary, and meaningful change.

T. Michael White, MD, FACP
A HealthCare Value Professional
Author of *UnSafe to Safe: An Impatient Proposal*
for Safe Patient-centered Care

If you are a physician, nurse, healthcare executive, or other healthcare professional, read this book to understand how to actualize your calling to help others heal. But especially if you ever have been, are now, or might in the future be a patient, then read this book so that you will be able to recognize and choose a hospital that delivers the type of high quality care that you deserve.

Tommy Thomas, PhD
Healthcare Culture Transformationalist
Author of *The Power of Opposite Strengths*

"Listen to the patient; they are telling you the diagnosis."

Sir William Osler
"The Father of Modern Medicine"
(1849 – 1919)

In Memory of Alex J. Goldberg
Who died at age twenty-seven of a preventable medical error

April 29, 1984 – June 16, 2011

DEDICATION

This book is dedicated to every patient, everywhere.
With all the training we physicians, nurses, and healthcare professionals
have, what matters most to patients must drive every decision we make.
It is the most important thing we can do to improve healthcare.

ACKNOWLEDGMENTS

After decades of working in an industry that looks to checklists, handbooks, and binders full of operational "things to do" to solve its ills, exploring the idea that "the answer" is relational was quite the task to tackle, and impossible to do alone. My research consisted of two decades of boots-on-the-ground, front-line interaction where I accumulated my findings directly from the source. The tireless physicians, nurses, and managers of hospitals across the country shared their stories, frustrations, and challenges, while the patients I interviewed fought through their fear to honestly provide me with the answer to the question I asked hundreds of times: "What matters most to you?" The cast of the book is directly related to these anonymous participants in my journey, and I can't thank them enough.

I wholeheartedly thank my primary contributors to this book effort: my business partner Jonathan Long, my writing consultant Joel Kampf, and Richard Stern, our creative guru. Their insights and ability to give and take, with just the right amount of each, sure made my effort more effective...and my job a little easier. I couldn't have done it without them.

My reviewers consist of my colleagues and dear friends who never held back and gave me the most important thing a reviewer can share—the unabashed truth.

Many thanks to: physicians Deb Parsons, Jack Cochran, Joe Bujak, Larry McEvoy, Larry Levitt, Stephen Klasko, Randall Levin, and T. Michael White; nurses Sue Collier, Casey Blumenthal, Rita Gurian, and Keith Boyle; and executives Roger Seaver, Gordon Clark, Jeff Selberg, Bob Anderson, Miles Otoupal, Rulon F. Stacey, PhD, FACHE, Richard Umbdenstock, and Chris Osborn.

Thank you to Second River Healthcare—Jerry Pogue and Sierra Weese have been invaluable resources and moral support during my first foray into this new world of book publishing.

I would not have penned a word without the everlasting, all-encompassing support of my family. My mother, Roberta Wong, first planted the seed about me becoming a physician, and through her own perseverance and sheer force of will did everything she could to ensure my dream became a reality. To my sons, Evan and Will, who test me, remind me, and help me to be a more trusted parent every day—I can't thank you enough. Inspiration is hard to find if you have to look for it...which makes me a very lucky man as I need look no further than my sons.

In saving the best and most important for last, I give a Lifetime Achievement Award in Trust to my wife of thirty-five years, Cindy. I've been blessed to have a friend, a confidant, a companion, and a fellow traveler on this journey. She helped me understand the nature of total, unconditional trust that has proven to be the key to my personal and professional fulfillment. I owe everything to her love and support. I will never be able to say thank you enough Cindy—which won't stop me from saying it every chance I get. Thank you.

PREFACE

You may be asking yourself, "What's a physician doing writing a book about accountability and culture? Why isn't he writing about the issues that physicians and hospitals really care about...like safety, quality, or improving the patient experience?" The truth is, I have written a book about all of those top-of-mind issues and more.

As a physician, I was trained to look deeper than the symptoms and diagnose the root cause of the disease. As a healthcare consultant, I have learned to approach organizations we work with in much the same way. My many years as a physician, medical director, and consultant had me seeing the same pattern...watching the same repeating organizational symptoms substantially cost all of us: our organization, the physicians, nurses, our entire hospital culture, the community, and mostly, the patients.

So I just didn't feel it was enough to offer up temporary solutions to recurring symptoms. Instead, I've sought out the root cause of our overwhelming safety and quality issues, and in doing so, discovered where patient-centered care really begins.

You would think by the title of the book that I was anti-hero. Not the case. But after speaking with literally thousands of patients, I know that patients don't want hero doctors or nurses. Patients expect us to work as teams—that's what matters most to them.

But that's just not what's going on. The "I can do it better if I do it myself" or "Every man for himself" paradigm still rules in most of America's hospitals. And that translates into an unsafe culture that, in many cases, under performs and under delivers for patients.

When we look at the startling number of how many people die each year in the US from mistakes made in hospitals, not to mention all the preventable non-fatal mistakes, it's surely not because of lack of talent or technology. We have the best of both. It's surely not due to lack of commitment—I've been working on the front lines of diverse hospitals across the country for the last twenty years and have seen plenty of skilled, experienced, dedicated people. But what's truly unnerving is how the phrases "That's not my patient" and "Just do your job" are consistently said by a lot of these dedicated people, in almost every hospital I've been to. This is an industry-wide accountability dilemma. The failure to dismantle the silo mentality and create high-performing teams is keeping us from creating patient-accountable cultures. And it not only doesn't give patients what matters most to them—it's literally killing a number of them.

That's why I wrote a book on accountability and culture. The story is based on a "real life" incident, with characters that I've seen and met in hundreds of hospitals. It's designed for you. As a physician, nurse, or manager, you don't need any more binders full of initiatives or checklists. Yes, certain checklists are very good and necessary, but they won't get to the root cause of the problem. They won't help you diagnose the ills of your culture and cure them.

We're all operating at capacity—I understand that. We don't feel like we can add any more to our plates. And I'm suggesting we don't have to. *Heroes Need Not Apply* supports leaders and medical staff by offering clarity and direction on how to have the most impact on improving care without adding more to our workload. It sets the tone and gives you the context necessary to give patients what matters most to them.

You'll recognize our characters—they work beside you every day. You'll be a fly on the wall for their personal conversations, thoughts, dilemmas, and how they deal with the everyday challenges we all face. And you'll learn about the tools and strategies they use to gain the clarity needed to coach and lead teams toward building a patient-accountable culture.

Brian D. Wong, MD, MPH
CEO, Bedside Trust

FOREWORD

Healthcare today is often cast in dollar terms that are enormous and hard to process, especially with the complex models of reimbursement, risk sharing, policy application, access, referral patterns, incentive alignment, and a dictionary's worth of ever-evolving acronyms. Much of the discussion and much of the language move the debate, discussion, and ultimately the intention, away from what brought people to medicine in the first place—to provide people with the best possible care.

The story and intention of Dr. Wong's book bring us back to the core of what healthcare is about—the care of patients. The story will immediately engage anyone in the care system: physician, administrator, mid-level provider, nurse, trustee, and most especially, the patient. This work is a call to action to rise above the noise and politics. It asks us to recognize that out of the noise and challenges of reform, the only way to improve the system from top to bottom is to build foundational, trust-based systems infused with respect and communication, driven by service to the patient.

Mid-story, the key catalyst character asks, "Where does the patient come in your equation?" The line, and ultimately this fantastic book, ask the question, "Where does the patient come into the healthcare equation?" It is a question worth asking at each and every step of delivery.

We often hear the word "systems" in delivering care, but we're not just system operators. This book challenges the gracious, brilliant, talented, and well-intentioned members of our system to fundamentally change the way they operate. It challenges us all to go back to where we started and align our mission with the passion that created our purpose—to improve the lives, the experiences, and the outcomes of patients: to offer pathways that not only save lives, but also afford the patients the opportunity to change their lives with new pathways of behavior, treatments, and thus outcomes.

This story should first scare and then inspire. The storyline is unfortunately all too common. As resistance to new models grows and incumbency entrenches to protect "my" patient, "my" referral, "my" job, or "my" revenue stream...we lose patients. Systems fail when people's capability and great intention is stifled by poor communication or false transparency. Defending or legitimizing our position rather than solving the root cause of the problem is an easy trap. The answer Wong offers is not a simple "trust me" and "Kumbaya" culture, but rather a system infused with great leaders who coach, mentor, and behave in a manner that sets the norm for great intentions to be aligned with providing great care. Even the best can be better by investing in themselves as teams and re-dedicating to patient care with the by-product of great outcomes. We know this type of approach is sound. Neuroscience has demonstrated these connections. Financial results can validate the action in real dollars that are the by-product of better engagement, higher efficiencies, and lower turnover. More critically, patients are better off in this learning culture. Not only does the behavior of their caregivers change—theirs does too.

Service-driven culture requires humility to understand that where we are today is not yet good enough. We can collectively get better by any and all metrics, each and every day. Patients can and must receive value and the opportunity for enhanced wellness at each and every step of their journey through a system of care. The hero in this story can and should be the reader. We hope it is…

Rulon F. Stacey, PhD, FACHE
President & CEO, Fairview Health Services, Minneapolis, Minnesota
Past President, University of Colorado Health
Past President and CEO, Poudre Valley Health System
2008 recipient of the Malcolm Baldrige National Quality Award

Chris Osborn
Vice Chair of University of Colorado Health
Past Chair of Poudre Valley Health System
CEO, Coach Training Alliance

INTRODUCTION

Delivering the right care at the right time in the right setting is the core mission of hospitals. Yet, even the best hospitals experience preventable medical errors that result in patients being harmed. Now more than ever, hospitals must collaborate to design better systems to keep people healthy, make care more efficient, and reduce health problems after discharge. Hospitals, physicians, and post-acute care facilities must share information and implement best practices to achieve the best transitions, outcomes and value for patients. In essence, they must do everything they can to prevent errors—and many are, with their ranks growing daily. But, to ensure these efforts are successful, we must help all administrators, physicians, and nurses to utilize the right tools, strategies and cultures to foster teamwork, communication and accountability.

In Dr. Brian Wong's fictional story about the staff of Angels of Seattle Hospital in Washington State, we see what can happen when a series of errors and communication breakdowns occur. Through a compelling storyline and characters that every hospital employee will recognize, *Heroes Need Not Apply* examines the root causes of hospitals' most pressing safety and quality challenges. It offers practical strategies to improve communication among staff, dismantle silos, and build high-performing teams. We are reminded that every medical error is an opportunity to learn how the system can be modified, and how at-risk behaviors can be managed to significantly reduce the rate of harm.[1]

Heroes Need Not Apply is a timely complement to the gamut of quality and patient safety initiatives hospitals are undertaking. It brings a human element to the equation and underscores the importance of making patients and their families full partners in the care process. It illustrates the necessity of creating the right culture in a hospital to enable patient safety to reign supreme. Most importantly, it reminds us that when we focus on the ultimate and singular goal of providing patients with the best possible care, everything else will fall into place.

Dr. Wong draws from his wide-ranging experiences as a physician, medical director, and health care consultant to provide insight into how cultural issues at hospitals can undermine patient-centered care. As hospitals strive to improve the quality of care and to provide patients with the best possible outcomes, *Heroes Need Not Apply* is a great resource for every physician, nurse, executive, and board member.

Richard J. Umbdenstock
President and CEO
American Hospital Association

[1] Institute of Medicine. *To Err is Human: Building a Safer Health System.* Washington, DC: National Academy Press, 1999.

ONE

When Dr. Ben Waller saw Edie for the first time he had no idea he would be involved with hastening her death. After all, he was tasked with saving lives.

By his tenth birthday, Ben knew he would be a physician. When he wasn't playing the Operation game, or running off with his father's stethoscope and sphygmomanometer to check the neighbor kids' vitals, he was glued to reruns of St. Elsewhere on the tube.

He wanted to be Dr. Mark Craig with a touch of Jack "Boomer" Morrison thrown in. Who wouldn't want to be a superstar cardiac surgeon, while having Boomer's easy ability to connect with his patients? But from listening to how his dad worked with patients, he knew Boomer was a little too touchy-feely for the real world.

Since then, he'd realized that you need some of Boomer's bedside manner; but taking charge and saving lives like Mark Craig, that's where reputations were built. And having been in this game for five years, Ben knew that taking charge and doing things his way was the quickest way up the ladder.

And then he met Edie Worden. Her sweet, helpful way of seeing the world might have been obnoxious if she wasn't so genuine. A petite forty-year-old brunette, her life had turned upside down three weeks ago when an aggressive cold, or at worst a bronchial infection, compelled her to get a check-up and walk into his internal medicine practice at the hospital. It didn't take long to discover non-small cell lung cancer.

Ben referred her and her husband, Chris, to Dr. Hartley, one of the staff oncologists, who quickly determined that her survival depended on the removal of one of her lung's five lobes, which was scheduled for tomorrow morning with Dr. Ethan Lang.

Although thankful to Dr. Hartley for a fast diagnosis, Chris quickly snapped up his iPhone and googled Dr. Lang to check him out. After building his own business from a home office start-up to a nationally respected brand strategy firm, he knew the importance of vetting everyone he worked with. And he wasn't about to let just anyone operate on his Edie. The results came back with nothing but accolades. With almost thirty years of surgical experience, Dr. Lang appeared to have done hundreds of surgeries and was known as one of the best clinicians in the state. That eased Chris's mind somewhat, but the engrained skepticism of running a business for the last ten years had him thinking, *We'll go with this guy, but I'm going to shadow his every step.*

Dr. Ethan Lang, the number one admitter to the hospital, past chairman of the Department of Surgery, and present chief of staff, currently sat on more boards than the parquet floor at Boston Garden, including his present position as head of the Medical Executive Committee (MEC).

Ben had quickly moved up the ranks to become the head of Internal Medicine and become a full voting member of the MEC, all due to his relationship with Dr. Lang. Although difficult for Ben to admit, Lang, or more specifically his network, had been his meal ticket since he walked through the door. Lang introduced and supported Ben's new practice at Angels of Seattle with the unspoken caveat that Ben would feed Lang's surgical practice and generally bring work into this hospital. The hospital sometimes felt a little like a realty firm, where referrals are everything. And if you weren't onboard with Lang and his "You scratch mine and I'll scratch yours" network, there was only so far you could go at Angels. Lang was known to never send a colleague a referral again if they didn't heed his advice.

Part of Ben actually admired how Dr. Lang took over the room the second he walked through the door. He'd never thought about it going in, but getting respect here was no different than in medical school, where you ran around obsessed with fear, 24/7.

So far, Ben had managed to keep on Lang's good side, although Lang had no idea that Ben was considering dropping his practice and working directly for the hospital. It was just getting tougher to make a buck. With shrinking Medicare reimbursements, it was getting too expensive to do it all on his own. Although he was catching up with his loans to some degree, even the minimal office upgrades, like transitioning to voice-recognition dictation and dealing with ongoing staffing issues, were taking their toll on him.

He'd once thought that he'd be successful if he just did a good job taking care of his patients. But with running the office and the financial struggles, he still couldn't afford to live the way he wanted to. And the answer always came back to seeing more patients. He began to wonder if he shouldn't have taken another career path to begin with. His friends in the corporate sector made a fortune with far less stress. He found himself constantly asking, *How did I end up struggling like this?* This wasn't how things were supposed to pan out, but he still loved medicine and believed he could do some good and eventually, make a good living.

Dr. Ethan Lang would not be a happy camper if he knew Ben was thinking about giving up his practice and (in his words) joining the dark side...along with almost half of the current physicians working at Angels. Ben brought it up in passing once and Lang barked, "Nobody's telling me how to practice!"

Lang believed that when competition was removed from the equation, along with it went choice. Ben didn't know what to think. But one thing he knew for sure: there was almost a fraternity-like self-protecting culture here, and it paid to belong. He once heard Dr. Hartley refer to the "White Wall" and asked him about it. Dr. Hartley explained that just like the fraternity of police officers have a "Blue Wall"—a code of backing each other up no matter what, physicians who were in Dr. Lang's inner circle semi-seriously considered themselves surrounded by an invisible White Wall. And financially at least, it paid for Ben to get inside.

Although Lang could be a jerk a lot of the time, Ben had to admit he was an excellent surgeon. He took things to the limit sometimes, and that made a lot of people, especially legal, uncomfortable. But you couldn't argue with his results. His practice was one of the best in the city and his surgical reputation remained sterling.

Ben caught up with Edie and her husband Chris just after she checked in. Walking into the room he said, "How you doing, Edie, Chris?"

Chris piped up first, obviously nervous as all get out and feeling the complete lack of control that goes with this new territory, "It's kind of a mixed bag. It's scary and a relief all in one. We've been pretty much a mess, but as long as things are moving forward, it's okay, I guess."

Edie sat up in bed with that constant smile beautifully masking her fear. *I can't help wondering if I would handle things as gracefully as she does. Probably not.*

She quipped, "Hey, Doc, you guys have your knives all sharpened and ready to go?"

"Yes, Egor is in the back, bent over a sharpening stone. You doing okay, Edie, you have any questions or concerns?"

Still putting on her "not a care in the world" face, she said, "Just make sure you and Dr. Lang don't have too many cocktails tonight. There's nothing worse than a sharp knife in the hands of a dull surgeon," which they both laughed at a little sheepishly.

Ben tried to set her at ease, "No worries, Edie, your surgery is pretty straightforward and Dr. Lang has done hundreds of them."

Chris joined in, "I'm sure you guys can get the lobe out, Doc, it's whether or not it's metastasized that has me worried."

Edie burst back, "Come on, Chris, I thought we decided to cross one bridge at a time. If we start worrying about everything that could go wrong, we'll go nuts. Remember, we have to positively project."

"It's pretty easy to imagine the worst," Ben said, "but there isn't any value in it. Right now, this moment, that's what matters. You're totally right, Edie, you're doing yourself a big disservice if you don't think positive."

"You're right, Doc," said Chris. "We don't need to waste any more time worrying about things we can't control."

They bantered for another few minutes and Ben headed out thinking how lucky they were to have each other. And how lucky she was for coming through Ben's door. Although he wasn't operating, he felt his quick catch may have saved her life, and setting her up with Lang was great for him, and for Edie too. Jerk or not, Lang could cut.

TWO

Although he wouldn't be at Edie's surgery, Ben always felt a little anxious for his patients. He wished Mel were home to help keep his mind off tomorrow, but it was girls' night out, and although he could've used the diversion, he might as well welcome the solitude.

After just six months of dating, Ms. Melanie Swift had moved in with Ben. She was real big on wanting a guy who could talk openly about anything, which continued to be Ben's biggest challenge with her. It's not that he didn't want to talk to her openly and honestly, it's just that he'd never been very good at it, and the medical school experience didn't do much to help him along. Since becoming a physician, he'd learned not to depend on anyone. If you want something done right, do it yourself. He wished she could understand that, but if you haven't experienced medical school, then you didn't have a clue about the responsibility and vulnerability physicians experienced. You couldn't go through it without feeling like everyone was gunning for you.

As a physician, he'd been trained to internalize and pretty much fly solo. By trained, he meant that everyone does it, so it must be right. He knew that he had to strongly believe in himself. Ego was definitely necessary.

Granted, Dr. Ethan Lang's ego was a gargantuan pain in the butt, but how can you possibly have the wherewithal to make life-changing diagnoses and operate if you didn't believe you were the best man for the job? Ben knew from the start that he sure as heck wasn't going to depend on somebody else when it came to making a life-or-death decision.

Right now, he was trying to figure out whether to let go of his practice and work for the hospital. Part of him would like to hear Mel's take on it, but something compelled him to follow his instincts and experience and decide for himself. It was all he really knew.

THREE

Nurse Melanie Swift spent the last few minutes before her shift sipping coffee on the hospital steps and feeling the subtle warmth of the early morning sun. She began to steel herself for the trials of her shift. Even though a large part of her day revolved around managing her nurses, she would never give up working the floors, knowing she would be lost without daily patient interaction. Remarkably, she had the hardened battle mentality the floor required, without ever letting go of her *Florence Nightingale* spirit which had drawn her toward nursing in the first place.

Like most every other nurse, Mel admired Nightingale for what she did while nursing soldiers during the Crimean War. In a man's world, she took things into her own hands. As soon as she realized that the lack of hygiene was killing more soldiers than battle wounds, she quit applying more "Band-Aids," and went straight to the core of the problem. She had the sewers cleaned and the ventilation repaired, and the death rate dropped nearly in half.

Mel couldn't help but wonder what it took to fight through the bureaucracy one hundred fifty years ago and really get something done. Here was a woman who raised enough funding to open the first secular nursing school in the world, and Mel had to fight tooth and nail to get most of the physicians at Angels to let her finish a sentence, much less listen to her advice.

The sun felt so good, she struggled not to look at her watch, which she really didn't have to do anyway. By now she could feel when it was time to get in there. But she just couldn't get Ben off her mind.

She loved her work. That was a given. But just thinking about her relationship with Ben made her excited...although there was always a little nervousness that accompanied her delight. She felt a real attraction to the guy, but worried that his good attributes were taking a back seat to his ego maniacal perception of what a physician should be...according to his mentor, Dr. Ethan Lang. What a jerk.

Being under Dr. Lang's wing made it hard for Ben to see anything with his own eyes, much less his heart. But that's where she saw herself come in. She shook her head and wondered if she could ever separate herself from being a caregiver at work and in her personal life, and immediately admitted she couldn't. Then a nurse on her shift rushed by, reminding her she'd better get in there.

Her first task of the day would be preparing Edie for surgery. Mel was on a first-name basis with most of her patients because she wouldn't have it any other way. And when she made up her mind you might as well just get out of the way and give in. There was no telling her what to do.

Mel was all about the patient...period. Physicians, for the most part, were too overwhelmed and self-absorbed to think about putting the patient above their own needs. Sure, there were a lot of good ones, but most of them acted like they were sitting on some pretty high horses. The ones she called her friends seemed to be the ones who based everything on what their patients needed.

That's why she was still nervous about Ben. She was certain that he was capable of honestly opening up or she wouldn't have moved in with him. She really believed his good qualities far outweighed his *I am a physician and you're not/You don't have a clue* mentality. She knew he was crazy about her, but a part of him still saw her only as a nurse. And she had to break him of that. She could tell that sometimes he just pretended to listen to what she was saying when she went on about work. Those were the times she just wanted to knock him out.

She once told a physician, "If you just listen to what your patients have to say, they'll diagnose themselves."

But very few of them listened to her—she was just a nurse.

Edie had her best face on when Mel walked in the room, "Morning, where's Chris?"

Edie formed a soft smile, "I sent him down to the cafeteria to get something in his stomach. He slept in the chair and hasn't eaten in I don't know how long."

Mel answered, "How lucky to have found a guy like him. How about you?

You need anything, you okay?"

"As okay as I can be," she shared. "To be honest, I am pretty damn scared."

"All I can tell you," said Mel, "is that Dr. Lang may lack the kind of bedside, or nurse-side manner he should have, but they call him Golden Hands for a reason."

Edie shot back, "You talking from experience?"

"Thanks...I just threw up in my mouth."

Edie quipped, "You probably have your hands full with Doc Waller anyway."

They both chuckled when Dr. Ben Waller walked through the door.

FOUR

Ben was always pretty amped on surgical days even though he wouldn't be in the OR. He went through his routine of getting up early, taking a run, brewing a cup of coffee, and sipping it in the bath while reading the paper. By the time he walked through Edie's door, he'd been up for hours, gone over his appointments for the day, performed early rounds, and would now give Edie a little confidence boost.

Melanie stood beside Edie's bed, totally in control of the room. Ben tried to hide his fondness of Mel from Edie. Yes, Mel was pretty, fit, smart, and had the mouth of truck driver when necessary—and she was unbelievably sure of herself—but it was that undefinable chemistry that took over every time he saw her. For a guy who prided himself in being in charge of things, Ben had less and less self-control when it came to all things Mel. His heart rate increased every time he laid eyes on her.

Her patients were lucky to have her. He thought, *If I'm ever a patient in this place, I'd want Mel to take care of me.* Even being a manager didn't keep her from getting her hands dirty every chance she could.

"Good morning, ladies." They both smiled and returned his greeting.

Mel became all business, "Dr. Waller, I'll be prepping Edie in a few minutes. Are you and Dr. Lang on schedule?"

Ben couldn't help but smile, knowing that Mel kept everybody in this hospital accountable, one way or another, "I checked the OR and believe it or not, they're actually on time."

Edie chimed in, "Where's Doctor Lang?"

Before Ben could even process the thought, Mel answered. "He'll drop by for a second right before you go under. He thinks he's a conductor or something. He likes everybody standing by with their instruments waiting for him and then he makes his grand entrance."

Ben tried to soften it a little, "He's just going through his pre-op ritual and getting focused. No need to bother him until we need his magic hands."

Leaving the room, Ben felt Mel's eyes boring a hole through the back of his head. He knew she wasn't happy about his covering for Lang, and believed that Lang should have been here himself. Ben thought, *Covering for a fellow physician, if I want to be brutally honest with myself, has become the natural thing to do. Especially because this guy really is my meal ticket.* He thought that Mel would understand how it all fit together after working with physicians for years.

Ben believed there was no way he'd have made it this far if he just said what was on his mind. Being a physician isn't about telling the truth or not—it's about showing up and doing what you need to do, trying to get good results, and not getting in any trouble along the way.

Even when he was a UCLA undergrad working completely unmonitored with study groups, he kept it close to the vest. That's all he'd ever known. Ben grew up in a house where things were better left unsaid. His father was a strong believer in "Figure it out for yourself if you want to learn anything."

His folks were pretty good about having dinners together most nights, but it wasn't filled with very much "How was your day" banter…just a lot of his dad's complaining about the incompetents, and pass the salt please. But with all of his complaining, Ben's dad had a thriving practice and his patients seemed to love him. Ben knew that's because he got results and dedicated most of his time and life to it. How to act became apparent very early in life. Monkey see, monkey do.

FIVE

en found Dr. Ethan Lang in the surgeon's locker room slipping on his scrubs.

"Dr. Lang, there's still time to see the patient before surgery. She's in 2304."

Dr. Lang brushed him off, saying, "Listen, Waller, I have no time for hand-holding, that's what nurses are for. I'm going to cut out a lobe and save her life. Don't you think that's enough?"

And he abruptly walked out the door, knowing that Ben couldn't argue with that or anything else he said for that matter. And it struck Ben as odd that he didn't even want to.

Ben walked by the surgical suite noticing that Edie was already prepped and ready to go. In this hospital, starting a surgery on time was half the battle. With so many consistent screw-ups, some surgeries started two to four hours late. Ben slipped into the gallery for a few seconds.

The nursing staff looked animated through the glass, but as soon as the surgeon walked in, the banter drained from the room.

Dr. Zeller, the anesthesiologist, was reading the chart and making his calculations when Lang made his entrance.

The surgical nurse, Julie, whom Mel had taken under her wing, approached with the PET scan images, saying, "Here you go, Dr. Lang. Here are her most recent images."

Lang shot back, "If I wanted them I would have asked. I've read Dr. Hartley's notes and I don't need any more info other than I'm removing the right inferior lobe (RIL). Hell, it's written right on her. Now let's get this done before I fall behind today."

Ben had also read the oncologist's charts and there was no mistaking the diagnosis for removal of the RIL. But Nurse Pain-in-the-Rear wouldn't back off.

She pleaded, "Dr. Lang, I beg your pardon, but I took a look at the scans and it looks like the tracer showed damage to the right superior lobe."

"Dammit, I've worked with Dr. Hartley for twenty years and I'll trust his notes over a nurse's scan diagnosis any day of the week. Just do your damn job or I'll get someone else who will."

Ben stood there frozen. He knew any nurse that was cleared for surgery had seen a ton of scans. But he also saw Hartley's notes, and Lang had done hundreds of these without an error. What kind of an idiot nurse would tell someone as powerful as Lang what to do? He might be an ass most of the time, but he knew his stuff.

Once the cutting was under way Ben headed back to his office for a pretty standard morning, knowing that his quick catch and Lang's good hands should give Edie a great chance at a normal life, if the cancer hadn't metastasized.

He headed down to the Angel's Café to grab a cup of coffee between patients when he ran into Mel. He decided not to bring up what he saw in the OR—if she didn't ask, why should he say anything?

She approached him as if on a mission and angrily said, "Ben, did you hear what happened to Edie, your patient?"

"No, but I'm sure if Lang had had any problems he would have told me. I saw him heading into a meeting a minute ago and he didn't say a word. Why?"

"You know Julie, the surgical nurse I'm mentoring? She just came by in tears. She insists that Lang took out the wrong lobe."

Immediately Ben sprung to his defense, "No way, Mel. He's done a hundred of these surgeries."

"I know, Ben, but this time I think he screwed up. Julie's really good at what she does, she's seen a lot of scans and insists that Lang took out the wrong lobe."

"Sorry, Mel, but she isn't a doctor, so I wouldn't worry about it."

Mel responded, "Great answer, Ben. Dismiss her because she's just a nurse like me."

He tried to break in, knowing that he'd immediately crossed onto thin ice.

She continued, "But this time she may be right. She said the lobe he took out was pretty pink and spongy for a bad lobe. She didn't see any dark spots or anomalies."

He countered, "Did she see both sides of it? Did she touch it to check its elasticity? Maybe the scan picked it up early and the spots hadn't surfaced yet."

"You don't get it, Ben; the scan highlighted the superior lobe, not the inferior. She is sure of it and I believe her."

He didn't know what to say. If she was right, and she almost always was, Lang made a huge mistake at Edie's expense.

But he couldn't even think about being a part of that right now, so he said, "Mel, I trust in Lang and Hartley, and what's done is done. Tell Julie to do her job, stop worrying, and everything will be fine."

"Fine, Ben," she said.

As she stormed away he couldn't help thinking that he really admired her grit, but sometimes she needed to be put in her place if this relationship was going to work. He thought of her as a nurse and himself, a physician. Case closed. Not to mention the fact that he could never see Lang leaving anything to chance when it came to self-protection, or protecting physicians in general. If Dr. Ethan Lang had one mandate in life, it was keeping physicians safe.

SIX

The rest of the day just blurred together. Ben saw eighteen more patients and walked his afternoon rounds.

He didn't have to try hard to avoid Mel. She was pretty busy between surgery and recovery, and they thankfully missed each other most of the afternoon.

Then, while walking to the locker room before heading out, he suffered a head-on collision with a category 4 fury.

Mel wasted no time. "What in the hell is wrong with you? Is it that I'm a nurse, a woman, or what? Or do you treat everyone like they're invisible?"

He tried to answer but couldn't. He could tell that it took a lot of effort for her to compose herself when she said, "Look, Ben, after seeing the scan myself, and running it by some of the techs, I know that Lang took out the wrong lobe. Any minute now, the lab's going to confirm it."

Instead of actually thinking about what she said, he shot back defensively, "Come on, Mel, you really shouldn't be saying things like that about Dr. Lang without solid proof."

She replied, "Is that what I should be focused on, Ben, covering my ass with the good Dr. Lang? What do you think I'm really talking about here?"

"You're saying we still have to remove the bad lobe and Edie's going to have incredibly diminished lung capacity. I get that, I'm just not convinced there's a problem."

Her tone seemed to almost soften. "Yes, first and foremost this is about Edie. But after that, and I mean right after that, we need to talk about why something like this can happen in the first place."

"Look, Mel, that's all fine, but let's make sure something happened. I was about to head out to run a couple of errands, but I'll slip by the lab and see if they're done, and then we'll know whether we have something to talk about. And when I disprove your theory, maybe you can reconsider and eat a little humble pie for dessert tonight."

"Thanks, Ben," she said. "We'll see, smart guy."

Ben didn't know why he retreated from the room feeling like his tail was between his legs. Lang should have looked at the scan, but dammit, he'd earned his spot here, and although Mel and Julie were pretty sharp, they weren't physicians.

By the time he reached the lab he felt less confident. He gave the lab guy the patient information and he returned in less than a minute and handed Ben the report.

The first word Ben saw was "Benign." The lobe they removed was no threat to Edie's health or life. And that meant that the malignant lobe was still in there, slowly killing her.

He didn't know if he looked "kicked by a horse" pale, but he sure felt it. He walked over to a folding chair, sank down, and closed his eyes thinking, *We just cost that sweet woman a great deal of her ability to breathe and totally screwed up her quality of life.*

After re-reading the report he asked to see the slides and the remaining lobe tissue.

Damn, Julie and Mel were right. All he could wonder was who was going to take the blame for this?

SEVEN

Ben called and paged Lang three times before he eventually called back. "This better be good, Waller," he said. "We're headed out the door."

He told him.

"I don't believe it," he said. "What a crock. You better go back to that lab and make sure those grunts got it right. I double-checked the notes again after the surgery, and I know I took out the right lobe."

Ben said, "But it looked pretty pink and elastic, didn't it?"

He shot back, "Listen, Waller, you don't always see malignancy on the surface."

And then Ben finally found his backbone and forcefully said, "Look, Dr. Lang, I read the lab report, I went back, double-checked, looked at the slide and the remaining lobe tissue. You extracted the wrong lobe."

Dr. Lang went quiet.

And then, "I'm coming in. Get the slide, the tissue, and the paperwork and meet me in my office in twenty. And keep your mouth shut."

The line went dead.

Thoughts circled his head like a windmill gone crazy. *Should I contact administration? Legal? Oh great, am I screwed here or what? No matter who's to blame, only the hospital and physicians have malpractice insurance, so it's a safe bet that Lang would top the list. After all, physicians have the most exposure, and Lang did the cutting. But what about Dr. Hartley? It was his report... surely he would have some liability?*

His thoughts circled back to CEO Jane Carolli. After a nursing career she topped off with becoming CNO, she finally achieved her goal of getting the CEO position when her predecessor was fired by the hospital board after a vote of no confidence from Dr. Lang's Medical Executive Committee (MEC).

He had no idea how she was going to react to this. All Ben knew about Carolli, and most administrators he'd met, was that her bottom line probably revolved around budgets. He'd never actually had much of a conversation with her outside of a meet and greet. When he did see her, she seemed pretty distracted and maybe a bit overwhelmed.

What Ben saw as overwhelmed, Jane Carolli experienced as frustration associated with figuring out how to navigate in managerial waters as the top dog. More than up for the task, one of her biggest day-to-day struggles centered around leaving the CNO/nursing mindset in the past. For years as a nurse, Carolli, like all nurses, had to either ask physicians, or at least strongly consider how they would react to the choices and decisions she made. Not due to a lack of confidence on her part—it was just how the culture was— nurses asked, while physicians did whatever they felt necessary. Now as CEO, she finally held a post where she could act on her ideas and strategies without asking for permission.

But old habits do die hard. She was getting better about it, but it still slowed down her reaction times occasionally, which others might perceive as indecision. But that just wasn't the case. After years on the floor, Jane Carolli had big ideas of how she wanted to see the staff at Angels of Seattle evolve. She just didn't have the time she needed to work on a strategy with all the new fires that popped up daily. She figured she spent about 20 percent of her time actually leading the hospital, which to her meant changing how people worked with each other for the better. The other 80 percent was taken up with managing those daily fires. It didn't take her long to realize the difference between the two. Managing her problems—mostly having to do with staff—had nothing to do with what she considered leading, the opportunity to make some substantive cultural changes at Angels. With 680 beds and 1,575 physicians, she had her work cut out for her, but her mind was set on it, and "giving up" were foreign words she couldn't even pronounce.

But Dr. Ben Waller knew nothing of Jane Carolli's thoughts and struggles. He was pretty consumed with the first major medical mistake he was even peripherally involved in, and he couldn't let go of the fear that some of what was coming down the pike was going to land on him.

EIGHT

Lang didn't look as worried as Ben thought he would when he ushered him through the door. He sat down behind his desk before speaking. "Okay, Waller, before we make sure that we're on the same page, I need to know if you told anyone about this."

"No one but Julie, the surgical nurse, and nurse manager Melanie Swift know. Julie went to Mel for help and then Mel brought it to my attention, which prompted me to check out the lab results."

Almost stepping on Ben's answer, Lang asked, "Do they know the lab results?"

"Not sure. But I'm sure Mel will be checking for herself if she hasn't already. You're not thinking about covering this up somehow, are you?"

He said angrily, "What do you think this is, an episode of *Law and Order*? Of course not. But we have to lay this thing out for legal and Carolli. Look, Waller, there will be a full Never Event Investigation and we'll be sued. This is why we have malpractice insurance in the first place."

Lang continued, "Now let me see the sample and the slide."

Ben handed it to him as he swung his chair around to the microscope. He didn't make a sound, re-read the report, checked out the remaining sample, and just sat quietly for a moment.

"It had to be Hartley," Lang said. "Although I've never known him to screw up like this, his notes were clearly wrong. I need to talk to him before we do anything else."

Ben couldn't help himself, "But shouldn't we tell Legal and Carolli right away?"

Lang answered, "I'll call Carolli tonight and we'll talk to her in the morning together, to make sure our ducks are in a row. In the meantime, tell no one."

And then, the unfortunate afterthought came to Ben. Unfortunate because of the circumstances; but on a personal note, really unfortunate that he didn't think of it first thing.

He felt depressed as he quietly uttered, "What about the patient? What about Edie and her husband Chris? They'll not only need to know, but she'll need another lobe removal ASAP."

"Tell them nothing tonight. Why get them more worried and all stirred up in the middle of the night when she's still foggy from recovery? It can wait until morning."

He went on, "Just don't do a thing, Waller," and then paused for a second "will you see Swift and that other twit?"

"They'll probably be seeking me out anyway. How do you want me to handle them?"

Listen to me, thought Ben, *I am already "handling" people.* He began to feel like he really was in a *Law and Order* episode and not real happy about the side he landed on. It wouldn't surprise him if Jack McCoy walked through the door any minute.

"Listen," said Lang, "you're not going to change anyone's mind about anything. After all, she was right. But you can ask her to wait through the night and assure her the patient will be told first thing in the morning. Tell her that I am in the process of rearranging my schedule to fit Edie into surgery in a couple of days, as soon as she's a little stronger. Now beat it."

Ben retreated, not at all thrilled about having his tail between his legs twice in one day, not to mention his impending conversation with Mel. He thought he'd just let her tell Julie.

NINE

He shuffled pretty slowly toward the nurse's station, not in any hurry for Mel to rip into him. He knew she was due to leave, but was pretty sure she had stuck around for him.

This was not what he needed right now. He couldn't help thinking how this could potentially add to his workload. *Okay, calm down.* Even though it wasn't his fault, some of it could stick on him, which might not be good from a meal-ticket perspective.

He turned the corner and saw Mel, knee on the floor, tying a shoe for an older guy in a wheelchair. That pretty much summed up Mel. It was no surprise to find her doing that, whether she was on the clock or not.

He came up behind her, feeling like Bambi sneaking up on King Kong.

"Mel, are you free?"

"Yes," she said as she snapped around, "I've just been killing time waiting for you."

Timidly he said, "Will you meet me around the corner at the pub and we can talk over a beer before we head home?"

All business, she countered, "What did you find out, Dr. Waller?"

"Great, now it's Dr. Waller. Mel, please, meet me at the pub in ten minutes and I will tell you everything."

She replied, "You've already told me plenty, but okay, I'll see you there."

He turned and practically sprinted for the door.

Ben was already sitting at the bar with a pitcher of beer and couple of glasses in tow, when Mel arrived, poised to speak. He immediately cut her off, "You were right, Mel. I saw the slide and the sample and so did Lang."

She tried to interrupt but he kept going, "I know what you're thinking, we need to tell Edie, but what good will that do tonight? She's foggy and in and out of consciousness. Just let her rest for the night and we'll all tell her tomorrow."

On a roll, he continued, "Dr. Lang is already juggling his schedule to set up another surgery, and he's getting to the bottom of what happened with Hartley's notes. The guy might be an ass half the time, but he's not evil and he wants to make things right."

"Make this right?" she said indignantly. "How are we ever going to make this right? Lang just wants time to circle the wagons. He doesn't give a rip about Edie and what's in store for her now. And what about Julie? She was scared to death and never spoke up her entire career until now. And knowing Lang, she'll end up under the bus. Granted, she's naïve and hasn't picked up on the fact that a lot of docs and nurses eat their young around here, but she doesn't deserve this."

Ben weakly countered, "I'm sure she'll be fine. You'll straighten her out. She'll get it. Listen, Mel, maybe it doesn't look like it from where you stand, but Lang is here for his patients. That's why he's so successful in the first place. Sure, it seems like he's circling the wagons, but you have no idea the pressures he...we feel every day. How can you blame him? The last thing we need around here is some kind of witch hunt. How would that benefit Edie or anyone for that matter?"

He kept going, "I just don't know how this happened. I can't imagine Hartley screwing up this badly. If only Lang had listened to Julie and checked out the scan."

Mel answered, "You just don't get it, do you? This is much bigger than not checking the scan; this is about everyone running in five hundred different directions. This is about fear, Ben. A nurse's fear after being slammed and shut down by physicians every time she tries to share an idea or opinion."

"Wait a minute. Granted, this place could use a little improvement, but this was about a mistaken oncology report, period."

Ben thought, *She's going a little off track. Either Hartley or someone on his staff screwed up. Yes, Lang could have looked at the scan, but if the report was correct in the first place, we wouldn't even be having this conversation.*

Mel continued, "What did he say to Julie in surgery, Ben? Wasn't it something like, I'll take this report over any scan diagnosis from a nurse."

He probably should have thought before answering. "I know Mel, he was wrong, but you have to look at his and Hartley's history and experience. This was an anomaly, nothing more."

And even as the words spilled out of his mouth, he couldn't help but second-guess himself. But he felt he had to stand his ground and back up Lang. After all, it was their asses that would likely be sued, not hers. Nurses had it easy in that regard. The MEC's "White Wall" was making more sense by the minute.

Mel spoke very deliberately, "Ben, we'll get to the bottom of what happened with Hartley's notes in the morning. And I get that this wasn't planned or intended. But Edie is going to suffer greatly because Lang has no respect for anyone who's not a physician."

She doesn't get it, he thought, but he knew where Lang was coming from. These nurses didn't have to go to school for eight years and barely live through the internship/residency nightmare. Physicians *should* put themselves on a pedestal. They not only make life and death decisions every day, they have to live with them.

She continued, "How are we nurses supposed to do what we know is right and use our own judgment when everyone else is running around like headless chickens? Every day I see a bunch of nurses second-guessing themselves because a lot of the docs treat them with total disrespect. Lang just took it to a new level today when he told Julie to just 'Do her damn job.' She knows how to do her job, Ben."

He broke in for a second, trying to gain a little ground, "You guys do great work, Mel. Everyone knows that."

"Bull, Ben," she countered. "But that's not the problem. I know how to do my job, but I'm working in a vacuum. It's like everyone has their own personal mission and we're not even working under the same roof."

She paused for a second before saying, "I tell you, Ben, if you spent a day following me around watching everything I do—and for that matter, if I spent a day shadowing you—you know what we'd probably find out? We'd find out that everything both of us does greatly affects how everyone else around here does what they do."

What she said kind of made sense to him. But as a physician, it seemed like every day greeted him with new career-threatening potholes to fall into. So why wouldn't physicians take whatever road was safest for them? Hospitals were only as good as their physicians. The support staff was just that—support. Since Ben didn't have a death wish, he would never say that to Mel. Plus, he always had the one hundred and fifty grand in debt he had to pay off in the back of his mind, and without Lang getting him voted on the MEC and opening the door to the referral network for him, he'd be screwed.

Instead he said, "Mel, I hear what you're saying and I get it. But I think we should find out all of the facts about today before we dissect the entire hospital. Fault will be found and someone will pay for it. Until we know the answers, there's just not that much to say."

The disappointment on her face couldn't have been more palpable when she said, "Ben, you're acting so much like Lang in some ways it's scary. How did you get so cynical? We'll wait to see what happened when they convene the Never Event Investigation. But, Ben, no matter who pays for whatever mistake was made, their price pales in comparison to the cards Edie's been dealt. There has to be a better way. In a perfect world, I'd spend all of my time seeing patients instead of handling all the redundant administrative stuff sent down from upstairs. I spend way more time at my desk then necessary, when I should be at the bedside. But that's how it is, has been, and will always be."

The conversation, thankfully for Ben, segued into meaningless drivel for a few minutes until he made a lame excuse about checking on a patient he had admitted earlier in the day. There was no use in scurrying home with her. Neither of them wanted to talk and he knew he'd see nothing but her back facing him in bed all night, so he tossed out a twenty-dollar bill, and got out of there as fast as he could.

He was in no mood to debate hospital culture and hear about the trials of being a nurse. He really believed he loved this woman, but she just didn't get it. Let her step into a physician's shoes and feel the responsibility and she'd probably realize how lucky she really was just being a nurse. She could just do her job and go home. She didn't have a clue.

TEN

Even knowing what the day would bring, and not having any contact with the woman sleeping inches away from him, Ben slept like a baby. His world could fall apart around him, but he could always sleep and eat.

He slipped out of bed about half an hour before Mel's alarm went off, and headed for the corner coffee shop instead of his usual stay-at-home routine. At the hospital, instead of dropping his stuff in his locker, he went straight to Lang's office. Knocking once, he plowed through the door, shocked to see the not-so-welcoming face of Jane Carolli...the mountain coming to Mohammed.

Lang continued to pace as Carolli opened with, "Well, Waller, you couldn't wait a little longer to get your feet wet?"

Before Ben could come up with something that didn't sound pitiful, she continued, "This is the deal. It turns out the radiologist's original PET scan diagnosis was correct in identifying the right superior lobe. But Dr. Hartley, a great diagnostician, is a dinosaur nevertheless, and still writes out his notes by hand." It turned out his assistant, Jerri, was culpable as well. It was Jerri's job to translate Hartley's chart notes into digital documents so they could be sent via e-mail to a hospital or lab when necessary. His writing was stereotypically physician, but she was pretty good at deciphering his scrawl.

That day, she struggled. His notes said that the patient needed immediate removal of one of her lung lobes, but the description of which lobe was overly messy and smeared. She knew it was the right lung, and could make out the letters "erior" at the end of the word, but the first few letters were illegible. She googled "lung lobe" and found an image that showed the five lobes, and she realized that it was either the "inferior" (lower) or the "superior" (upper). She showed it to his nurse who couldn't make it out and told her to ask the boss.

Knowing that this guy yelled more than she was used to, she wasn't thrilled, but she had little choice if she wanted to be driving a convertible Mustang by summer. So Jerri knocked on his door, went in, and asked if he would take a look at the chart. He didn't bother to look up when he bellowed, "Get out of here and do your job."

She said, "Please, Dr. Hartley, I just need you to look at one word I am having trouble with."

"If you can't do your job, I'll find someone who can."

As she walked back to her workspace she kept seeing herself headed down the coast highway and figured that someone else would probably double-check later down the line, so she guessed...wrong.

When Jane Carolli paused, Ben let slip, "You're kidding me?"

She looked at him with definite annoyance and just shook her head no.

She swung around in the chair facing the window. "For now, here's what is going to happen. Since the hospital has the deepest pockets, Dr. Hartley and Dr. Lang will probably be sued, and you, Dr. Waller, will probably be called to testify. I've scheduled a meeting for tomorrow morning at seven for you two to sit with counsel. I'll deal with the rest of the surgery team personally, and then we'll begin to sort this thing out when we start the first Never Event Investigation (NEI) in a week or so. My new vice president for medical affairs will be here, and I'll see about getting him to run the NEI."

Before moving on, she almost imperceptibly looked toward Lang for his approval, not knowing that Ben caught the glance.

She continued, "For now, you two will have to go tell the patient. You tell her we went by the oncologist's notes and that I am looking into that right now. Then you make it clear that your only priority is to get out the bad lobe and get her better. If they talk about a lawsuit, tell them that I will be coming down later in the afternoon to talk about it. Ethan, you have to deflect the blame elsewhere, so she'll have enough faith in you to get the job done. Clear?"

"Yeah, yeah, yeah," said Lang. He was already thinking, *A Medical Executive Committee meeting needs to happen as soon as possible. Wagons need to be circled and the White Wall needs a fresh coat of paint.*

"Come on, Waller," he barked. And they were out the door, both en route to get their rounds out of the way and meet up at Edie's room to deliver the second worse news a physician ever has to give.

ELEVEN

M el heard and felt Ben get up and wanted to roll over and say something to him. She wanted him to at least own up to the fact that things shouldn't be this way and that the Langs and Hartleys of the world had to be held accountable. Unfortunately, she saw a lot of those two in Ben, but believed he could grow past that. He was a good, kind man who had fallen into a trap that seemed almost impossible to avoid. Some realized it and made course corrections and others forged through a self-centered career, inflicting collateral damage along the way. From the beginning, she believed Ben would see this and eventually make good decisions. She wouldn't have moved in with him if she didn't believe that. But he was slowly but surely becoming part of Lang's overprotective White Wall. She needed a man who could talk to her about anything, any time. But if he couldn't even open up his mind about work, how could she expect him to really open his heart to make this relationship work?

As she approached the hospital, she ran into Julie sitting on the steps, clinging to her morning latte.

Looking down at her feet, Julie muttered, "This is the first morning since I began nursing that I am afraid to go through those doors."

"Why? Do you think it's going to be any different in there today than yesterday? There are people who need you in there regardless of what else is going on."

"I just know this whole thing is going to fall on me."

"Buck up, Julie."

"Mel, why are you being such a jerk to me? You understand what these guys are doing more than anyone. Why are you taking such a hard line?"

"Julie, it's not just these guys. What about Jackie, the nurse that came down on you up on three? Or Cathy on our floor? A lot of nurses in this place don't give a rip about you or me. Do I let that affect how I do my job? No, I just come in with the mindset that I am here for the patients and if someone isn't willing to help me, then that's their problem. You can't let others block the road for you."

"But this whole Edie deal is going to fall on me."

"Look, Julie, I've been glad to show you the ropes around here, but you have to grow up. Do you think you're the first one this has ever happened to? Just about every nurse with some years here has their own horror story, and they survived by growing thicker skin and concentrating on their patients. This will mainly fall on the physicians and the hospital."

Julie kept staring toward the ground until she finally let it all out, "Mel, I did everything by the book. I followed protocol, and I know what I'm doing. I read the radiologist report on the scan and then took a look at it. I saw the abnormality right away and knew it didn't match the diagnosis. I tried my hardest to point it out, but Lang just shut me down. I went through the entire surgery knowing it was wrong. I don't know if I could ever speak up again."

Mel felt her pain and the dissonance that overwhelmed her, but knew that going down that road would take her nowhere fast.

"I know. You got screwed. And I do care about what's happening to you, Julie—I just know that the only way you'll get through this is to grow up and stop whining. We all feel sorry for ourselves sometimes, it's natural, but there is no value in it whatsoever. Now let's get our butts in there and take care of the people who trust we're going to do just that."

TWELVE

Edie looked pretty good when Lang and Ben entered the room. Even Chris was beaming. Mel busily checked the bandages and obviously hadn't said a word. Ben didn't know that Carolli had already spoken to Mel, since she would be the first to interact with Edie.

Mel averted her eyes and continued dressing the bandage when Dr. Lang put on his poor excuse of a smile and began to demonstrate his best bedside manner.

"How are you doing this morning, Edie?"

She answered, "Pretty good, I guess—why don't you tell me?"

Lang said, "That's why I'm here."

Then he came closer to the bed but still in a position to talk to both her and Chris, saying, "Edie, the best thing I can do for you is to tell you exactly what is going on without pulling any punches."

Ben could see both Edie and Chris deflate, looking to each other for comfort.

Chris blurted, "What are you talking about, has the cancer spread?"

"No, Chris, not that I know of," said Lang. "Edie's lungs and the surrounding tissue looked very good. In fact, when we took out the lobe, it also looked very good. And it turns out that it was."

Edie sat in shock, and Lang continued before Chris could say a word, "I went by the oncologist's notes and it turns out that the report specified the wrong lobe."

A seething Chris started in with, "You've got to be kidding me. After all Edie's been through, you guys can't even get a chart right."

Not knowing what possessed him, Ben entered the fray, "Chris, Edie, we read the chart right, it's just that the chart was wrong."

Neither of them knew about Lang not checking the scan, but Mel did. She had just finished on Edie and was standing behind Ben. He could feel her eyes drilling holes in the back of his head.

And then Edie spoke, "Wait a minute. You're telling me that the bad lobe, the one killing me, is still in me?"

Lang jumped on it, "Yes, and it's our first priority to get it out of you. I've rearranged my schedule to get back in there tomorrow morning. I'd like you to rest one more full day before we go in. We still need to be aggressive about this."

Edie was about to say something when Chris cut her off, "Why should we trust you again? Edie, we need to move to another hospital."

Edie looked at Chris adoringly and said, "Chris, we can't just blame these guys if they were given a bad chart, and I need this thing out of me. I am staying here."

Everyone stood hushed for a moment when she continued, "But, Doctor Lang, what does this mean for me...for my recovery? I know the lung only has five lobes and that I was going to be left with about 64 percent lung capacity after one removal...at least that's what Dr. Hartley said."

Lang answered without pause, "I don't like to put numbers on it, as everyone's different. Yes, when you have a lobectomy you'll have diminished capacity. It will be harder to fill up your lungs with air and your ability to exercise will be curtailed significantly. But first and foremost, you'll be alive, you'll be able to do things...you'll just have to be more measured and take your time."

"And there are breathing exercises you can do to improve things," Ben said rather lamely.

"Breathing exercises," said Chris, "You've got to be kidding me. Edie, I'm calling Larry Dodd and asking him to come down here and give us some legal advice before we meet with administration. These guys made the kind of mistake that would put my company out of business...and we're talking about your life here. If you want to have surgery tomorrow, fine, but I have to do something. I just can't sit back and hope they get it right this time."

Chris stood up, looking lost, turned and kissed Edie, then left the room.

Edie said, "Schedule me in for the morning. I want to get this over with." And she painfully turned away from them.

Ben turned to retreat from the room and saw Lang had already disappeared out the door. Avoiding Mel's eyes, Ben couldn't even imagine what was going through Edie's head at the time. He couldn't believe she didn't get angrier, like Chris. Maybe she was just too scared to be angry.

When he turned into the hallway he almost bowled Lang over.

"Waller, don't talk to anyone until after we have our MEC meeting. I'm calling an emergency meeting of the committee for tomorrow morning before Edie's surgery. I'll let you know the time."

He about-faced and left in a flash. Ben couldn't help thinking, *Great, I can't talk to anyone and I live with the nursing manager most involved with the case. Well, I'll talk, but I don't have to tell her about the MEC meeting...we physicians have to stick together.*

THIRTEEN

Ben headed down the hall thinking that Lang's surgery was a no-brainer for him, and White Wall or not, somebody was going under the bus for this and it wasn't going to be him. Although Lang would never throw a fellow physician under the bus, it would solve a lot of problems if Hartley took the fall. Lang wouldn't hesitate to throw Julie under, or maybe he would say that she never said a thing. *Great,* thought Ben, *nobody else in the room would dare call him a liar, except maybe Mel. No, Lang's pretty arrogant, but not a liar.*

Ben headed back to his office when he got to thinking about how to best fit in at Angels. He eventually had to decide whether or not he should give up his practice and work for the hospital directly. It would clear half the administrative stuff off of his desk and give him more patient contact, but he knew Lang would pitch a fit. Of the 1,575 physicians at Angels of Seattle, 650 of them were employed by the hospital. Although Lang had great relationships with some of those who opted to (in his eyes) give up their autonomy, he vehemently opposed Ben going in that direction every time the subject was broached. And now, Ben was seeing firsthand how it might be wise to be under Lang's and the MEC's wing when everything hit the fan. It sounded much better than being on the other side of Dr. Lang's wrath. It all came down to autonomy and independence. He just didn't know if it was worth all the stuff Lang would throw at him, and worth all of the money troubles that would multiply without all of the referrals he received from being on the committee. To Lang, being employed by a hospital was like being owned— either you were a captain of the ship or a lowly mate waiting for your next orders. Ben wished he could talk to Carolli, but he had no idea if he could trust her, or anyone for that matter.

And with shrinking Medicare reimbursement he couldn't really afford to lose all of his referrals right now. Although he knew Lang couldn't care less about him personally, he was a card-carrying member of the physician fraternity, and as long as Ben kept feeding the MEC members referrals, Lang would make sure they returned the favor. Ben knew where his bread was buttered. He was in a financial position that would have taken more than twice as long to achieve on his own, and by Lang bringing him onboard, it gave him a level of status a physician of his age could never have achieved on merit alone. A lot of the nurses, minus Mel, seemed just as afraid of Ben as they did of Lang and some of the other MEC docs. Rank really did have its privileges.

Ben just didn't know how this Edie episode would affect him. He knew Lang would do everything he could to make his life miserable if he found out he was thinking about working directly for the hospital. He would go ballistic if he found out he was even minimally checking out his options, and might even try to find a way to dump some of this mess on him. But almost half the physicians in this hospital couldn't have it all wrong. When Ben spoke to some of them, all they did was rave about how much less stress they felt since they gave up their practices. Ben didn't know how he'd do it, but he was sure he wanted to look into it further. But he knew he needed to make sure he stayed under Lang's protection at least until this NEI was over and done. Although part of him hated kowtowing to anyone, he kept reminding himself how lucky he was to have landed under this oppressive but influential protection.

The rest of the day was pretty straightforward. He saw to his patients, did a couple of hours of paperwork, and kept to himself. Normally, he would have checked on Edie, but he couldn't bring himself to stand in front of her. He knew he had to eventually, but he kept putting it off until he was ready to head out for the evening. And he almost went home without stopping by, when he ran into Mel on his way out of the locker room.

"Hey, Ben, where have you been hiding all day?"

"Just busy with patients, Mel. How was your day?"

They made small talk like everything was fine, thinking, *Aren't we medical professionals great at compartmentalizing?*

She smiled slyly and said, "You're not going to start talking about the weather next, are you?" Then, "Have you seen Edie this afternoon? I've been a little crazy and could only stop by for a few minutes around lunch."

"No," Ben lied, "I've been slammed with patients since I saw you this morning. I was on my way to drop by there on the way home tonight."

"Great, I'll go with you and we can go home together for a change."

They started toward Edie's room in an uncomfortable silence until Mel said, "Ben, let's grab a bite out tonight and get some of this stuff behind us so I don't have to sleep with my back to you all night."

Remembering what Lang had said in the hall, he didn't want to hash anything out, but he really did love this woman. He just didn't know if he could give her what she wanted. His medical career had to come before everything. But he hoped that didn't mean that he couldn't have a relationship, whatever that was. He chuckled to himself, *Maybe medical school should include Relationships 101 in the curriculum. Fat chance.*

He said, "Sure, let's grab a bite," in spite of the conversation he would have to navigate through.

They reached the room and saw Edie resting. *Thank goodness,* thought Ben. Then Chris called out as he walked out of the restroom.

"Hello, Ben, where have you been all day?"

Between Chris and Mel, he might as well have a target on his back. Ben answered, "Hey, Chris, it's been a pretty busy day. I just wanted to see how Edie was feeling."

"More scared than ever. We both are. For some reason I can't grasp, she seems to trust Dr. Lang, regardless of the fact that he screwed up the first time. I still haven't gotten any real explanation of what happened to Edie, but it's obvious that a lack of communication had something to do with it. Heck, if everyone in my firm worked in a vacuum like you do here, we would be dead in the water. Are you guys so focused on doing your own things that you can't even have simple conversations with each other? Have you ever even heard of teamwork?"

Ben really had nothing to respond with. *Not only did we all screw up, he doesn't even know the half of it.*

"Chris, they're in the process of putting together an investigation, so let's just concentrate on getting Edie through tomorrow, and everything else will come out in the open in the next few weeks. They're bringing in the new vice president for medical affairs to run the investigation. I'm sure we'll get a clear picture of what happened. But again, let's just concentrate on Edie right now."

Chris responded, "Okay. Our attorney said I shouldn't really be talking about this with you or anyone else in this hospital anyway."

Then Mel said, "Chris, when Edie gets up, tell her we were both here and we'll return first thing tomorrow. Edie's surgery is scheduled for seven-thirty in the morning, and we'll both be here a couple of hours before that."

Chris said, "Tell me the truth, Ben, even if the surgery goes great and they don't find any new cancer, what kind of shape will she be in when she gets out of here?"

"Everyone's different, Chris, and Edie's proven to us that she's extremely resilient, so I'm sure she'll have some struggles, but if anyone can adapt and make it work, it's her."

Chris shook his head back and forth as if he knew that Ben was hedging. "What does 'make it work' mean? Please be more specific and don't pull any punches. Edie's asleep and I have no desire to tell her anything that would worry her."

"Okay, Chris. Edie will have very diminished lung capacity. At first, she may not be able to walk for more than a few minutes without losing her breath and needing to sit down. But with time and work, she can improve. She'll be extremely susceptible to infections. A simple cold or exposure to any flu virus could cause serious problems. What was once a small inconvenience could now develop into a life-threatening condition. That said, with therapy, preparation, and a lot of positive energy, you guys will eventually be able to do most of what you want, as long as climbing mountain peaks isn't on your bucket list."

Ben was about to add that with a little luck she could live her normal lifespan, but his deer-in-the-headlights feeling made him realize he should just shut up. Seeing Chris's eyes beginning to water up and the reality of what lay ahead take hold, Ben didn't know what he should say or think.

If he felt any anger toward Lang or Hartley, then he had to blame himself too. He was one of them. And although he always wanted to be doing what he was doing, this part wasn't what he had pictured in medical school. He had always believed the patient should come first, until he realized that physicians are every patient's best and only real hope, and were pretty much justified in doing whatever was necessary to get the job done. Maybe physicians sometimes put themselves first, and kept a definite line between them and the patients, but that was necessary to keeping their clinical objectivity in place. Ben found himself questioning everything all of a sudden. In just ten seconds, he saw Chris turn from an aggressive corporate CEO to a bowl of jelly. For some reason, that had him terribly rattled.

Chris turned to both Ben and Mel, saying, "I'm still going to find out what happened here, but for now, I better start thinking about getting our house and our lives ready for Edie."

Mel added, "Chris, a lot of this is attitude, and Edie's attitude is joined with yours at the hip. I know it's impossible for you to let go of your anger, but I really suggest that you work on compartmentalizing it. When you're with Edie, things need to be enthusiastic. When you deal with the ensuing legal mess, do it without her. She'll know that you are angry, but she doesn't need to see it every day. She's going to have to steel herself to the fact that minimal movement will lead to exhaustion. Life is going to be harder before it gets easier, and she needs your positivity to help her get through."

"I know, you're right. I just feel like beating the crap out of someone right now."

Ben said, "Chris, everyone always talks about taking life one day at a time, but now that's what you're being forced to do. Let's concentrate on getting Edie through the next surgery. And I'll put you in touch with our respiratory, physical, and occupational therapists, along with the dietician, so you can begin putting together Edie's rehab program. Nurse Swift is right, when you're with Edie, you need to keep it all about moving forward."

"I appreciate what you're saying."

Ben saw his out, "We'll be here early before the surgery to check on Edie. We'll get through this together."

He said his goodbyes as he and Mel left the room.

FOURTEEN

It wasn't raining, so Mel and Ben walked down the hill to the Pike Place Market to grab a drink at the Alibi Room. Hidden below the hollering fishmongers and tourists, its out-of-the-way location gave the mostly local clientele a discreet place to melt into after a tough shift.

As they walked down Pike Street, Ben thought, *How come we physicians are such a tight-knit group, yet we don't even understand each other? If we didn't have medicine to talk about, we wouldn't have anything to talk about. Chris's expectation of physicians talking about everything and working in teams seems a complete fantasy. We weren't trained to do that and that's why we work solo.* He could barely imagine it any other way, when Mel responded, forcing the realization that he was thinking out loud.

"Wouldn't that be a kick in the pants? Maybe there's hope for you after all. Have you ever thought about what it would be like if we acted as if we were all here for the same thing?"

"Aren't we all here to take care of patients?"

"Maybe, Ben, but most of the people I work with are more about covering their own asses than anything else."

Ben couldn't argue.

She went on, "But how can you expect a bunch of people to change when you and I are so superficial in our relationship?"

"What do you mean? I may not show it the way I should, but you know I do care a lot about you, Mel."

"I don't doubt your romantic intentions, Ben, but we have different ideas about what respect means. I know you admire or at least appreciate how I do my job, but, do you respect me and the other nurses as much as you do another physician? It doesn't cut both ways you know, either you respect me or you don't."

Ben knew what she wanted him to say and he knew that it wouldn't be the truth. He got that nurses were critically important, after all, they were on the front line. But at the end of the day they were here to follow physicians' orders.

"Look, Mel, I think the world of your abilities and think more highly of you than most of my peers. It's just that I was brought up to believe and was taught that my training puts me on a different playing field. We both greatly affect our patients, but I have to make life and death decisions that begin and end with me. I'm the guy who has to live with a negative outcome."

"That's funny, Ben, I thought Edie and Chris had to live with what's going on at work right now, not you or I."

Touché. "You're right, Mel. But so am I. All of this training...my skills and dedication, they have to count for something."

"They do, Ben. But they can't be the excuse to treat people like dirt. They can't be the be-all and end-all of everything you try to justify."

Ben tried to change the subject, "Does this mean I'm on the couch tonight?"

She didn't answer immediately as they passed the disgusting, eye magnet gum wall under Pike Place Market, and arrived at the bar. When they sat down she said, "I won't be issuing the verdict quite yet. You have a pretty warped view of things from my perspective. But you do seem to have the ability to evolve. We can only hope you use it. Let's get some beer and see what happens."

FIFTEEN

When Ben attended his first Medical Executive Committee meeting, he had to pinch himself more than once. The MEC consisted of medical staff department heads that submitted proposed changes to the medical staff by-laws and elected members at large. They were a layer of protection, independently governed, that didn't have to answer to the hospital, per se. And although Jane Carolli attended most of the meetings, this was one meeting where she was not in charge.

Just weeks earlier, Ben had become Angels of Seattle's youngest-ever head of Internal Medicine. In a hospital with 680 beds, that was a pretty big deal. Everything started going his way during his first month in the hospital, when he ended up sending his first two surgical referrals to Dr. Ethan Lang. He knew of Lang's reputation as a surgeon—everyone did—and he remembered his father's only advice when he took the job: "Feed the top of the food chain and it will come back to you." Lang took notice and was particularly pleased that Ben didn't opt to work for the hospital like most of the new physicians. Ben's dad was right. Lang's network, his MEC members, started feeding his practice just weeks into his tenure. He wasn't sure why Lang eventually brought him onboard, but who was he to argue? Now, seeing it with the perspective of membership, he realized that Lang pretty much got what he wanted.

MEC meetings began with approval of minutes, and then usually went right into the credentialing report—who got on staff, and who got provisional-courtesy or active staff privileges. The members voted on who got "active privileges," and it was not doled out lightly. Now participating in such votes, Ben, like the rest of the department heads, followed Dr. Lang's lead. Ben knew where his bread was buttered. He was only a member because

Lang made it so.

Today's last-minute meeting felt different from the start. Jane Carolli wasn't there, and the normally talkative crew only murmured, waiting for Dr. Lang to start. Ben sat sandwiched between Dr. Hartley, Head of Oncology, and Dr. Sarah Lehman, Department Chair of Women and Children's Medicine. Also present were Dr. Bill Proctor, representing Imaging and Diagnostics, Dr. William Zeller from Anesthesiology, Dr. David Lee from Cardiology, Dr. Larry Simms from Gastroenterology, and Dr. Ida Hunnywell, from Emergency Medicine, one of the few MEC physicians employed by the hospital, due to Lang's disdain for all physicians working for the hospital. All of them were caught in the middle of a busy morning, but when Dr. Lang says jump...

"All right," said Ethan Lang, "I'll keep this short, but we need to make sure everyone is up to speed on a matter a few of us are dealing with. Unfortunately, due to Simon Hartley's idiot transcriptionist screwing up, and a novice nurse too afraid to get in my face, I was set up to accidentally remove the wrong lung lobe from one of Dr. Waller's patients. I hope to go in tomorrow to excise the correct lobe, and although the outcome is far from optimal, the patient should recover."

Although everyone in the room knew exactly how well Edie would recover—not very well—no one said a word until Simon Hartley spoke up.

"Like Dr. Lang said, it's becoming clear that my inept transcriptionist literally guessed when translating which lobe to remove. When Ethan stepped into surgery, he referred to my report and matched it with the markings on the patient's torso. He's been referring to my reports for twenty-five years, and this is the first time one was...well...all screwed up."

Ben couldn't help thinking, *Isn't anyone going to mention that the nurse emphatically pointed out that the scans didn't match up with the report twice, and Dr. Lang just blew her off?* But Hartley was looking down at the floor, and Dr. Zeller just sat there stone-faced. *That leaves me...and I may not know everything, but I know nothing good will come of this...it's not the hill I want to die on...the damage is done. And anyway, Hartley's transcriptionist really did screw up.*

Dr. Lang continued, "Yes, Simon, we all know we were both set up to fail by that idiot you hired, but the family will be coming after the hospital and us. I just wanted to make sure we were all on the same page when asked about it. As far as anyone is concerned, a person made a mistake and it cost her her job. Remember, this committee is the last line of defense for physicians. We're the most at risk and have to stick together. I just want to make sure our hard-earned reputation isn't tarnished. Anybody have any questions or anything to say?"

Nothing.

"Then I think we're done here for now. The new vice president for medical affairs is slated to begin next week, and according to Jane Carolli, he'll be running the Never Event Investigation. I'll bring him up to speed when he gets here. Meeting adjourned."

The group emptied the room faster than a crowd of shoppers racing into Target on Black Friday morning.

SIXTEEN

D r. Jack Martin began his journey to Angels of Seattle on Interstate 90 heading west through the Yellowstone River Valley, leaving Billings, Montana, in his rear-view mirror. Like Ben Waller's dad, Jack's father had set the stage for his medical career early on, and Jack never considered anything else.

He'd just finished up at St. Joseph's Hospital and Clinic in Billings where he started as an ER physician, loving the fact that good or bad, he could have a significant effect on patient outcomes on an hourly basis. There's nothing like the clarity that comes with immediate results. He then worked his way up to running the clinic, and then eventually became vice president for Medical Affairs of the entire organization.

Shortly after he started, for some reason Jack could barely fathom, his boss began to groom him for the leadership position. Later, after they became friends, Jack asked him why, and he said he couldn't really nail it down, other than he'd never seen anyone coach people like Jack did; he spoke slowly and asked questions that, more often than not, gave his team enough information to connect the dots themselves, this, combined with his encouraging tone, really got results.

He went so far as to say, "I've never seen anyone be so deliberate in how he talks to people—it makes them feel safe enough to respond. You don't seem to leave your relationships to chance."

Jack never looked at himself that way. He could only guess that he had his parents to thank for whatever his boss saw in him. His dad, and mom for that matter, acted more like coaches than parents. He grew up in a home where he and his sisters were encouraged to speak their minds—and they did—because his mom and dad really listened. They not only tried to understand them, but they actually used their ideas. They taught Jack that just because they were the parents, the elders, that didn't mean they were omniscient. They looked at everyone as a contributor—someone to learn from.

Although his schools did not foster an atmosphere where everyone felt safe to share their thoughts, he kept treating people the way he was treated as a boy. It was only natural to integrate his communication skills into his work relationships. That's the only way he knew to show up.

When it became apparent that he was going to become the next medical director of the hospital's clinic, he looked at it as an opportunity to effect even more changes.

His minor discomfort about transitioning from treating patients to becoming a suit kept him off balance at first. So when agreeing to the new job, he emphatically demanded a couple of days a week in the ER to keep his hands in it.

Before coming to Billings, Jack was a regional medical director for EmergeCare, with contracts covering sixty hospitals in a five-state area. It didn't take him long to see the common denominators everywhere he went, whether in a two hundred-bed hospital in Santa Fe or a twenty-bed rural hospital in eastern Wyoming. They all seemed to suffer from the same malady: a seemingly innate inability to get along and work together. And now he was on his way to the 680-bed Angels of Seattle.

As the interstate curved west approaching Big Timber, Montana, he looked at the Crazy Mountains in the distance and couldn't help thinking how their island-like appearance reminded him of what he saw everywhere—people working alone, as if they were the only ones in the building. It seemed like they were all incapable of looking in any direction but down at the floor after they punched in every morning. They might as well have been wearing blinders.

Reaching down on the seat next to him, he felt his pipe pouch and smiled, thinking about two of the biggest influences in his life, besides his parents. First was Ferdinand Foch, France's top general during World War I, who eventually became the supreme commander of the Allied Forces. A remarkable man who practically invented the "counterattack," Foch was interviewed and asked why he came out on top so many times, when he was seemingly outnumbered. He replied with something like, "When I have a tough decision to make, I smoke my pipe."

Jack immediately connected with Foch after hearing that. He figured out early that decisions were better made when you stopped to consider the implications of all options before responding to a question. Just a minute or even a few seconds could make the difference between failure and success, and in both their businesses, that meant lives saved or lost. Although it was easier said than done, you could learn it with time. The concept made so much sense to Jack, he started keeping a pipe around as a reminder and tribute to Foch's influence.

His other and even more significant hero was Dr. Viktor Frankl. The neurologist/psychiatrist did amazing things under great pressure, beginning with what he did while spending three years in a Nazi concentration camp. Frankl actually continued researching and practicing as best he could as a prisoner. He even created a special group to help new arrivals cope with the transition, and established a suicide unit.

Here's a guy who lost his wife and parents, felt impending doom every day, and wrote, "Between stimulus and response there is a space. In that space is our power to choose our response. In our response lies our growth and our freedom."

His captors took everything you could possibly take from a man. All they left him was his life and air to breathe. But he looked at it differently. He quickly realized that they couldn't take away how he responded to what was happening to him. Only he could decide how he dealt with his fellow captives and his captors. Besides being incredibly impressed with Frankl's cool objectivity in the face of absolute horror, his story immediately resonated with Jack as a physician.

All physicians know that everything begins with "Diagnose, then treat." But before you diagnose, you have to discover why things are happening by asking the patient. The better you ask, and listen, the more you know. Jack realized that the answer was almost secondary to the question. He discovered that it's not about speeding up, but slowing down and giving the patient time to pause, and smoke a pipe, and live in that space between stimulus and response.

Slowing things down became second nature to Jack. The Billings gang was a tough crowd at first, and Seattle, with over fifteen hundred physicians, would surely be a challenge, but if Frankl could use this method to his advantage in a much tougher situation, Jack figured he had nothing to complain about.

Once put in the position of power at St. Joseph's, Jack's approach to common conversation slowly but surely started to spread. Not only were people making more informed decisions, they began to listen better to each other.

And that small crack in the armor opened the door for people to pause, to begin looking outside of themselves for a minute, and to notice how much they affected each other.

When he found himself taking the time to really listen, it just validated that no one person, no matter how smart, was nearly as smart as a roomful of people. It became his mission to share this with everyone at St. Joseph's. It wasn't accepted by all, but eventually he won over the majority and started making some headway.

His new view from the top opened his mind to a world of possibilities. Although he missed being hands-on every day, he soon realized that as a "suit" he could do a lot of good on a much larger scale. And it all began with treating people like his parents treated him. *It's funny*, he thought, *with all that I learned in medical school, how come they left this part out?*

As he headed through the Bozeman Pass, he glanced to the right and noticed a small Appaloosa horse ranch. The serene setting had him thinking how much he would miss the calm of Montana as he headed into a hospital system that dwarfed the town he was raised in. He snapped back to the present and smiled at the thought of working with the 1,575 physicians at Angels of Seattle. He was definitely a little nervous. Although the number seemed daunting, he knew that it began with baby steps. It all started with a one-to-one relationship at the top, and building it out and down from there. No matter how big Angels was, one to one is the same everywhere.

SEVENTEEN

With the NEI review just three days away, Ben couldn't help but feel sorry for the incoming vice president for Medical Affairs. What a mess he was walking into. He thought, *Better him than me.*

Dr. Lang hadn't mentioned anything to him for the last week or so. Ben assumed Lang would do whatever was necessary to protect all the physicians involved, especially his old friend Dr. Hartley. When they last spoke, Lang quipped, "Hartley's given me more referrals than anyone in the hospital, and he's saved a lot of lives in the last twenty-five years."

Ben was pretty sure he'd come out of this fine, but something gnawed at him—something he couldn't quite put his finger on. He didn't know if it came down to the stress of his relationship with Mel, the decision on what to do with his practice, or just the normal stress that came with the job. Could he be suffering from the beginnings of burnout this early in his career? He thought, *"Come on, physician—heal thyself."*

He didn't talk to Mel about what was going to happen because he really enjoyed his time with her and didn't want to screw things up. She kept pushing her different perspectives on him, and although he agreed with a lot of her logic, for some reason, he kept coming back to the fact that he was a physician and she wasn't. Time would tell how things would play out.

Mel seemed pacified by Edie's successful second surgery and her robust rehab effort. Although Chris was still gung-ho on the lawsuit front, he had settled into his role as Edie's biggest cheerleader and caregiver, putting his work and everything else in the backseat. Mel couldn't help wondering what it would feel like to have someone believe in her so strongly.

Ben practically ran into Mel as he turned the corner heading for his office. She had been up and out of the house before he even stirred that morning. He felt his face light up when he saw her...and then immediately deflate when her somber expression came into focus. He never really saw her down about anything—angry yes, but not down.

"Ben, did you just get in?"

"Yes, what's wrong?"

"It's Edie. She was admitted last night with pneumonia."

He knew that could be a major problem with such diminished lung capacity, but according to the respiratory therapist, she was doing great with rehab. He was sure she would battle through it, until Mel finished.

"She died early this morning, Ben."

He immediately felt weak and feverish. What the hell? Even though he was young in his career, he'd dealt with his share of death. So why did he need to find somewhere to sit down?

As he turned to walk away, Mel was saying something that came across like the trumpety "Wah, Wah, Wah" of Charlie Brown's teacher. He just kept going.

He couldn't understand why this hit him so much harder than the other deaths he'd experienced. Sure, Edie was an exceptional person who didn't deserve what had happened to her, but things happen. It wasn't his fault, which brought him back to Lang. He really had to know what Lang was planning, and how he could end up on the right side of this whole mess. He had to talk to Lang and make sure his ass was covered. As he continued walking the halls in a zombie-like state, he began to realize why he was feeling so much conflict. Here he was worried about covering his butt, and he had almost forgotten about Edie...and Chris. He wondered, *What am I turning into?*

EIGHTEEN

Jane Carolli knew when she became CEO that people were going to die on her watch. And she also knew that people would continue to die, no matter how well she led. After years of nursing and her recent stint as CNO, the realities of medicine were nothing new to her.

She'd come to reluctantly accept that Dr. Ethan Lang was always going to act like he had the upper hand over her, thinking that he had the power to manufacture a no confidence vote from the Medical Executive Committee. She couldn't compete with his established network, but she'd already made some inroads with some of the MEC members and would work her butt off to gain the confidence of everyone on her staff. She just wished she didn't have to; it's not as if she didn't have enough to do with just managing things around here.

She wasn't sure how the dots were connected, but felt sure that Edie's death had to be related to the fear grip that Lang and some of the others had spread through the hospital. *Damn,* she thought, *I don't have any options other than to keep managing what needs managing, moving my agenda forward, and positively projecting the future.* Although she felt so swamped with problems that she could barely make out the tunnel, much less any light at the end, she knew one thing for sure, she didn't work her way up to this position to sit on her rear and take orders. Regardless of the hurdles and the fear Dr. Lang tried to generate in her, she was going to make a difference here whether her tenure turned out to be six years, months, or minutes. It was the only way she knew how to work and the only reason she was sitting in the big chair.

She started running through it again...Edie's husband, Chris, had already begun a lawsuit. Now he would really go to town. Lang might blame it all on the scrub nurse Julie, but nobody could believe that this was any one person's fault. Plus, although he could be a jerk, that seemed way too far-fetched for a man of his experience and dedication. Julie wasn't the only one with a big problem. Everything that happened had fallen into Jane Carolli's lap.

But Jane had some support coming in the form of her new vice president for Medical Affairs, Dr. Jack Martin. He would surely relieve some of the pressure and free her up to really press her leadership agenda instead of mostly managing people and putting out fires. And when it came to her agenda, she hoped he was the catalyst she'd been looking for. She had some pretty good ideas, but didn't know how to package them into something that was actionable...and then she met Jack.

She'd met him at a recent conference. They had a couple of drinks and a very refreshing and positive conversation. He seemed genuinely interested in his work. The discussion inevitably turned to sharing the challenges both leaders faced. Jack had dealt with the same kind of problems Jane had, but on a much smaller scale.

Jack somehow managed their conversation without really saying much. And what he did say was almost always in the form of a question...reminiscent of how her life coach worked. She found herself thinking and speaking about things she usually kept to herself because of the way he asked, and his insistence that she take her time before answering. Speaking with him felt different. He had a way of making her feel like he was safe to talk to, that he wasn't judging her. When she asked him something in return, he always hesitated before answering. They weren't awkward pauses—just a few seconds to really think before he replied. The guy really listened, and the few times Jane shared a couple of ideas, he seemed to really ingest them and genuinely think about them. Jane thought, *"How weird that I'm so impressed with what should be normal behavior."*

They talked about the Lang-like personalities he'd come across, and how he never fought them or considered them adversaries. Of course, Jack was a physician himself, so he could speak their language and connect on a level she couldn't. But he said that being a physician had nothing to do with it. He shared Viktor Frankl's stimulus-and-response idea and how he used it to get people to approach conversations the way he did. Jack shared how he'd always heard the old cliché *think before you speak*, but Frankl made the idea real for him. He started looking at his response as a valuable choice he could make—and why wouldn't he take a few seconds to think it through before sharing it?

When he really thought about it, he realized that it all began with listening. How many times had he been busy planning the next thing he was going to say instead of listening to what was being said to him? For Jack, Frankl's idea was a primer on how to have a conversation: how to listen, and how to pause and think before offering a response. Once he started doing it, he saw people relaxing and chiming in less defensively. So he took the idea throughout the hospital and clinic, and slowly but surely, people began feeling safer when it came to expressing themselves. This led to people working together in teams, which only months before had seemed impossible. And although it sounded like a fairy tale to Jane, Jack's boss confirmed it. He continued to tell the story of changes at the St. Joseph's Clinic, which only made her feel more excited. *And let's face it,* she said to herself, *excitement is not one of the emotions work generally inspires.* As she sat bewildered in thought, Jack said, "Jane, what do you think matters most to your patients?"

Caught off guard, she began to blurt out her first thought when Jack held up his hand saying, "Wait a second before you answer."

She thought for a moment and then said, "To feel like they're in a safe place—that everyone is looking out for them, and of course, to get well and get the heck out of the hospital."

Jack considered her answer.

"What do you think will make them feel safe?"

"I'm not sure."

"Jane, does it make sense to you that every patient's frame of reference begins with us...the people who surround them?"

"Sure, go on."

"I just talked about how Frankl's idea relates to having a conversation that invites people to engage...safe conversations. Do you see where I'm going with this?"

"I think I do. You're saying that if the staff feels safe, if we create a safe environment to work in, then that will funnel down to the patients. They'll see it and then feel it."

"Exactly. And you know, Jane, this listening exercise relates to a lot more than conversations. When I heard my boss sharing his frustrations, I realized that slowing down to listen and think before responding had everything to do with what he was going through."

"What do you mean?" asked Jane.

"He was consumed with getting things done—fulfilling his lists—you know, managing people and their problems. He was always looking for the quickest answer...to develop another Band-Aid to treat a symptom."

"I get that, Jack. We leaders are all in the same boat. There aren't enough hours in the day to deal with all the stuff that comes up. What else do you expect us to do?"

"I got him to do the same thing we just talked about concerning how you have conversations. I convinced him to stop and listen to what people were really saying and not planning out his response ahead of time. When he started taking the time to listen, pause, and think about the implications of what he was about to say, his relationships started changing to his and everyone's advantage."

"How?"

"It began with injecting, 'Tell me more,' into his exchanges. And he sat back and listened. He realized that people needed to be heard. Nothing new, I know, but he made it come to life. He said half of his problems went away just from hearing people out and getting to the bottom of why they really came to talk with him in the first place. He encouraged and received participation."

"It sounds so simple, Jack. It's kind of like throwing the ball back into their court to get them engaged in solving their own problems."

"Right. And as a result, he had fewer problems to manage and more time to follow through on his leadership goals."

Jack then said, "Jane, I'd really like to tell you more about everything we've accomplished in Billings, because I am really interested in trying to implement these changes on a bigger stage, if that interests you."

Jane didn't know what to say. His story was captivating, but he had no idea what she faced back in Seattle. His success in a medium-sized Montana hospital and clinic wouldn't necessarily carry over to a place like Angels of Seattle. Angels was definitely "The Bigs," and she wasn't convinced he could make any headway there. But it seemed almost irresistible to try. She was frustrated with dealing with repetitive fires that needed extinguishing which monopolized so much of her time, and she was motivated to make some game-changing adjustments to how things worked...or didn't work, at Angels.

After a few more minutes of small talk, Jack got up first to leave, said his good-bye, and started to walk away. He then turned around and said, "Think about it, Jane. Everything we just discussed became a reality in Montana. And I truly believe we can do it in Seattle." And he turned and left.

Unbelievable, she thought, this guy is like Columbo with a stethoscope. And at that very moment she knew she would try to hire him...whatever it took.

NINETEEN

With the NEI review a day away, Ben felt like calling in sick for the week. Since Edie's death a couple of days ago, Mel seemed estranged from him. They slept next to each other, but not together.

He really didn't know what she expected of him, but thought there was nothing he could do about what had happened or how things were going to turn out. Going head-to-head with Lang over this would have no value whatsoever. He couldn't help Edie or Chris anymore, so he thought it best to just keep his mouth shut, put his head down, and work. Mel would come around after the NEI meeting when she saw that he was powerless to do anything.

The knock at the door had him taking a quick look at his Day Timer, seeing that he still had an hour before his next appointment. He hoped that it wasn't Mel, thinking that he just wasn't quite ready for her yet.

"Come in."

A forty-something suit in a lab coat walked in with a Cheshire-cat smile, "Ben Waller, I'm Jack Martin, the new vice president for Medical Affairs."

Oh great, thought Ben. *He probably wants to drill me about the meeting he is going to walk into tomorrow, and I'm definitely not up for that.*

"Jack, good to meet you, what can I do for you?"

"Can I sit and visit for a few minutes? I'm making a few quick introductions to break the ice."

For some reason, Ben didn't believe him. *Sure you are,* he thought. *You're just trying to figure out how you're going to cover your ass and see if I have anything that will help you get through the meeting tomorrow.*

"Come on in and have a seat. I have a few minutes before my next appointment."

"Thanks, I'm kind of blown away with the size of this place. The hospital I came from was mid-sized, although it was one of the biggest in Montana, but this place is immense. If they didn't have the color-coded floor lines to follow, I'd be walking around in circles."

Ben wasn't going to give him much, "Yes, it's pretty intimidating at first, but you'll get used to it. Sorry, Dr. Martin, but I only have a few minutes, maybe we can continue this later over a cup of coffee."

"Famous Seattle coffee sounds good, but a beer sounds better...and call me Jack. I just wanted to go around and ask a couple of questions to get a feel for who I'll be working with."

Ben wanted to say, You mean who you will be jousting with at the NEI meeting tomorrow?

Instead he said, "Okay, ask away."

"So tell me, Ben, what do you think matters most to our patients?"

Ben couldn't figure out if this guy was kidding. *Was this his backdoor way into the Edie conversation?*

He said the first thing that came to mind, "Getting out of here in one piece."

"Let me rephrase; what do you think patients most need from us?"

At that point, Ben figured this guy was a loser that Carolli brought in as a sacrificial lamb. Okay, he would play along, "They need assurance from us that everything will be okay."

Jack paused for a moment. "How can we give them that?"

"I don't know...keep them confident."

"What do you mean by confident?"

"I guess they want to trust that we're doing our best for them."

"Well, Dr. Waller, Ben, trust, huh...interesting. Who do you trust around here?"

"How'd we get to that? Well, what the heck, I guess I trust some of the physicians."

Jack Martin didn't say anything. He just sat there looking lost in thought. The lapse in conversation felt a little freaky to Ben.

"Okay Ben, I'll buy that. So you only trust physicians...and just some of them?"

"Pretty much. We're on the same team. Look, you know as well as I do,

Jack, physicians have to go through hell to get here. We have to be skilled, we need to get things done, and be totally dedicated. It's not just a job—it's a lifestyle choice from the beginning. And these guys are the best around."

"How do you know they're the best?"

"I just told you. They're extremely talented, educated; they execute, and obviously, are very dedicated. They're just damn good. But you know all this, you're one of us."

"So you see physicians as the real leaders around here?"

"What do you mean?"

Jack didn't answer. He just sat there. *This guy is killing me,* thought Ben.

"Yes, I guess if you mean that we lead the way. This place depends on us above everyone else. If that means we're leaders...so be it."

"Well, Ben, how do you see yourself fitting in around here? What part do you play?"

"Like I just said, I bring my skills in every day and try to save lives."

"So how's it working for you so far?"

Ben couldn't answer with Edie still so fresh on his mind.

Jack rose, saying, "Thanks, that really helped. I appreciate your time."

Ben was not thrilled. He wondered where Carolli found this guy, and to what end?

As he reached the door, Dr. Jack Martin turned one last time saying, "Hey, Ben, since I'm new around here, how about introducing me to a good pub and catching a beer with me later?"

"Sure."

And he left. *Sure? What am I thinking? Great, now I'm talking without the slightest forethought. Who's the idiot here?*

TWENTY

NEVER EVENT INVESTIGATION I

The only thing that surprised Ben about the attendees was seeing Carolli sitting at the head of the table. He was sure she would throw Dr. Martin to the wolves and let Lang have his way with him, but he sat partly obscured, toward the far end of the room, a foot farther from the table than everyone else.

Carolli sat there in her normal, hurried state, looking like she wanted a carnival-sized gavel to get attention and (in a more perfect world) bean a few of the participants.

Dr. Lang took the other head of the table, flanked by Hartley on his right and Dr. Zeller, the anesthesiologist, on his left. You could almost see their spears and shields supporting each other. In contrast, Julie, Mel, and Ben rounded out the table meekly. Ben was thinking that he maybe should have sat with the other physicians.

Carolli started out with her "business-as-usual" voice that barely persuaded Lang to stop visiting with Hartley.

"Thank you all for coming. Normally, our vice president for Medical Affairs would chair this meeting, but I wanted to give Dr. Martin a day or two to get his bearings. I told him to join in whenever he feels compelled."

All eyes shifted to the new physician, and he just smiled and said nothing, furthering Ben's belief that this guy might be a worthless addition to the staff. Ben couldn't put his finger on it, but there had to be something behind his inane prodding.

"We're all pretty upset whenever we lose a patient, especially when it's truly avoidable. As I stated in my report after the incident, and in my apology to

Edie's husband, we take full responsibility for what happened and will do everything we can to make sure it doesn't happen again. This meeting isn't about placing blame, it's about putting systems in place so that we never repeat whatever mistake was made."

Yeah right, thought Ben, *this isn't about blame. Then why is Julie looking like she's about to get thrown on the sacrificial altar?*

Cutting Carolli off in mid-sentence, Lang proclaimed, "Thank you, Ms. Carolli. But I believe that we need to make it perfectly clear that this was not a physician-caused error. Dr. Zeller, Dr. Hartley, and I cannot afford unfound blame that will affect our premiums and our reputations."

Carolli countered, "Again, we're here to validate the sequence of events and build in preventative measures, not to assign blame."

"Yes, yes, yes, I know," continued Lang, "but we already know what happened and since it wasn't due to physician negligence, why should physicians be forced to add more safety initiatives to our already overflowing plates?"

Mel didn't give Carolli a chance to answer, "Surely, Dr. Lang, since the notes were misinterpreted and the scan wasn't re-examined prior to opening the patient, some new precautionary systems could only benefit our patients and add very little to our workload."

Lang looked straight at Carolli as if the nurses weren't even in the room. "Jane, we all know that the surgical nurse is feeling partly responsible for this error and probably not too rational, so having the nurses here will only create a hostile environment. Why don't you meet with them later to let them know what we decide?"

Ben was sure Mel was going to explode, but she just sat there holding it in.

Carolli looked at Dr. Martin and got nothing back. Then she faced the nurses.

"Ladies, I promise to get to all of your concerns when it's appropriate. You will be heard. Now I would like to move on to a safety discussion, so..."

Lang looked through Carolli and said, "Jane, again, we really don't have the time to discuss or implement safety protocols that we don't need. I am sure that if we stop pussyfooting around who caused this and get it out in the open, we physicians can get back to our patients."

Mel sat in shock, Julie couldn't take her eyes off the floor, the new savior Jack was scribbling something—probably a grocery list—and Ben just kept shaking his head back and forth as Lang spoke.

Lang continued, "We know for sure that the spineless transcriptionist at Dr. Hartley's office made errors that set this whole thing in motion. She's been fired, and Dr. Hartley assures me that he has set up internal systems to make sure everything is triple checked in the future."

"And, we know that this nurse could have been more insistent about the scan…"

Julie broke in, "But I did mention it to you…you just ignored me. I followed protocol to a 'T'—I know what I saw on that scan."

"Jane, are you going to let a nurse interrupt me?"

"Julie," cautioned Carolli, "please let Dr. Lang finish. You'll have ample opportunity to talk with me one-on-one, later."

Lang almost smiled. "She handled it meekly…period. And I am not taking any more excuses from nurses. If they can't do their jobs right, maybe they should look into waitressing…where people don't die if you forget to hold the onions on their burger."

Part of Ben felt pretty bad that Julie was getting the brunt of it, when the transcriptionist had surely sparked the change of events…but the other part of him, the physician, got why Lang was going down this road. He had heard Mel's take on what Julie had said, and he believed her. And he knew Lang was wrong for shutting her down this way, and yet he just sat there mute and conflicted. He thought, *When it comes to physicians and nurses, physicians know best…don't they?* Mel seemed to know what he was thinking and shot him the coldest glance ever. Ben almost said, *Somebody please give me a local.*

Firmly in protective mode, Lang finished with, "Look, Jane, I don't think the nurse has to go or anything. She and the other nurses are the ones that need beefed-up safety measures. So now that we know exactly what happened, I can't see any other reason for being here."

And he started to get up, followed a beat later by Dr. Zeller.

Jane Carolli looked like her underwear was tied in a knot. On one hand she wanted to shoot the guy and let him bleed out; on the other, she knew he was a good physician and needed his cooperation, even though the thought of it made her nauseous. Remembering what Dr. Martin taught her about taking a moment, she sat for a few seconds, thinking that Dr. Martin hadn't even said a word, and she had really hoped that he would join her in the fight. But she realized she needed to give Jack Martin time to figure things out—maybe at the next NEI.

"Unless somebody has something else to say, I will have to agree with Dr. Lang. I feel that the best thing we can do is begin the process of gathering feedback for new pre-op safety guidelines and schedule a follow-up meeting in two weeks to develop an implementation plan. Thoughts?"

Lang was already halfway to the door with his fellow physicians in tow, while the rest of the group sat motionless.

"Fine," said Carolli, "I'll get back to you with parameters for safety initiatives and a date for our next meeting."

Ben practically flew to the door, unable to meet Mel's piercing stare. As he headed back to his office, he tried to process that poor excuse of a meeting, which led him back to his own shame. He thought, *Is Carolli really going to be satisfied with another checklist added to our already huge paperwork burden? Maybe we can call it the Edie Memorial Pre-OP Checklist.*

Lang was his consistent self; he sure showed Martin who ran this place. Ben realized how much he really needed Lang and his network, but he couldn't believe how Carolli could put up with this guy. You needed a backbone of steel and a barbwire lasso to corral physicians.

As he crossed the threshold into his office, Ben almost ran head-on into Jack Martin.

"Dr. Martin, how did you beat me back here?"

"Sorry, Ben, I didn't mean to startle you. I just wanted to get your first impressions after the NEI. Thought we could schedule that beer for later tonight."

Ben knew he meant that he wanted to know who's really running this place.

"Well, Dr. Martin..."

"Jack."

"Well, Jack, I don't know if tonight's the best night for that." *Or any night for that matter,* he thought.

"Look, Ben, I'm going to level with you. That meeting wasn't what I was expecting and I am trying to figure out how I can be most effective around here. I need to know if that's the norm around here and a few other things. Give a newbie a break will you? You do like beer, don't you?"

Ben realized that this guy wasn't going away. He seemed like an okay guy, but hashing out this whole thing sounded horrible.

"Fine, Jack, unless I get caught up in something that I don't plan on, I can probably get out of here by seven. Why don't you drop by around then?"

TWENTY-ONE

Jane Carolli felt like she was walking down the hall while trying to balance a couple dozen plates on her head. She realized that Jack Martin wasn't ready to take the lead yet, but she had hoped he might jump in.

She knew she had made the right decision in going along with Lang at this point, regardless of the slight feelings of ineptitude that came with it. She had to bide her time and be strategic. Jack was probably asking himself who really ran this place, and she couldn't really blame him. She was hoping he was the real deal, because having a leadership strategy based on just surviving wouldn't help her accomplish her goals or help anyone else around here.

Since taking over the reins at Angels, Carolli had been trying to figure out a way to turn around what first appeared to be a no-win situation. She finally had a chance to lead and hopefully make a difference on a scale she only previously dreamed about. Then how come she felt so dead in the water?

She was constantly thinking about how she could break through this culture of unwavering gridlock. She didn't get this far by being meek or succumbing to the old boy's network, but here she was, so inundated with managerial tasks that keeping her chin above water took up almost all of her time. She knew that all of the strategies she'd envisioned for Angels would never come to be if she had to go on with business as usual. And Jack Martin was not only willing to help, he was enthusiastic...and he made sense. She had to accelerate his influence.

She glanced around her office and the supposed prestige it granted, and her anger and befuddlement grew. She was tired of being a manager. She wanted to lead the way, and knew that Jack Martin's strategy would work. *Patience, Jane,* she told herself, *patience.*

TWENTY-TWO

For Ben, the rest of the day was uneventful.

He had no desire to rehash the meeting; he was ready to drink. Jack Martin had left a note on his office door saying that he had to run some errands and he would meet him at the brewery. When Ben entered the First Avenue entrance to the Market, he almost ran over a middle-aged tourist wearing a t-shirt that read, "If I Throw A Stick Will You Go Away?" Yes, Ben thought to himself, *I would.*

He went down the stairs into a packed Pike Place Brewery. His new "buddy" Dr. Jack had secured a couple of prime bar stools and waved him over.

"Hey, Ben, glad you could come. This place is pretty cool."

Though he'd never thought about it before, he had to agree. It lacked the hidden anonymity and charm of the Alibi Room, but Ben wasn't ready to bring Jack into his inner circle of more private watering holes quite yet.

The waitress came, and when Ben ordered a pint of the local Pale Ale she said, "You know our Pale is closer to an Amber. If you want something a little hoppier, try the IPA."

Ben shot back, "If I wanted a lesson, I would have asked. What I want is a Pale Ale. Is that too difficult for you to understand?"

Jack broke in, "Well, I actually needed the information—thank you very much, and please get me the IPA."

Her face almost immediately recovered from Ben's browbeating and she moved off to pull the beers. *Where did that come from?* thought Ben. *Am I really that guy...that ass?*

Jack started in with, "You catch more flies with honey, Ben," and continued, "so it seems Dr. Lang is quite the leader amongst the docs."

Ben was still incredulously questioning his own behavior when he replied,

"On paper, Jane Carolli is the big boss; only the board can trump any of her decisions."

He paused, "I know. But aren't all of us physicians leaders too?"

Here we go again, thought Ben.

"Look, Jack, I can't imagine this place being much different from the place you came from. Lang is the biggest income generator in the hospital. He's run or been on every MEC since the Triassic Period. He has power and does a lot of good with it. And maybe Carolli's just a little intimidated; she's occupied her position for less than a year."

"What kind of good are you talking about, Ben?"

"Well, when I first arrived, he gave his network the green light to give me referrals, and honestly, they have pretty much built the practice I have today. And, he's helped a lot of other physicians in the same way."

"And what's his motivation, Ben? After seeing him in action for the first time, he just doesn't strike me as the altruistic type."

Ben thought, *What am I supposed to tell this guy? My feelings toward Lang have muddled into a pride-guilt-disgust stew. I've never been real proactive on the business front, so I'm kind of proud for putting myself in the right position to build this practice in the first place. I may have to kiss some ass, but I get his protection in return. So how come I feel this guilt and disgust?*

Maybe it was just the beginning of a beer buzz, but Ben started to get a pretty decent vibe off of Jack Martin, thinking, *Maybe I'll give him a little heads-up and give the new guy a break.*

"Well, Jack, to be honest, I have some mixed feelings about how Lang operates, but I have to be a realist. His network helped me build my practice and pay off my loans. And my practice allows me to treat people on my terms. But even more importantly, Dr. Lang is clinically superior to any physician I've worked with. He has the best reputation in this hospital and is known city-wide. Everyone wants to be treated by him. He's a great cutter."

"That's interesting."

"What do you mean?"

"It just occurred to me, when you mentioned 'treating people,' that through the entire NEI meeting nobody talked much about the poor woman who died...I think Edie was her name. In fact, nobody said anything about patient needs at all. I understand about covering our own asses and checklists and all, but you would think that the patients would be the centerpiece of every conversation, right?"

"You know how it is, Jack. We are all here for the patients. But if we don't put in the time and energy to protect our rights and privileges, we won't be helping anyone."

"You're right. But just for the heck of it, do you think that any future patients will truly benefit from whatever initiatives come from the NEI?"

Ben couldn't believe what he was hearing. He thought, *Was this guy that naïve? He's focused on patients when he really needs to be concentrating on his own survival.* When it came to Jack Martin's tenure at Angels, he could see the sand slipping through the hourglass.

"I'd have to say yes, Jack. If we had been following a pre-op list making it mandatory for the surgeon to revisit the scan prior to opening up the patient, this entire event would have never transpired."

"You're right, Ben. I guess I was wondering what we could do to avoid this type of thing before it reached the operating room."

"You're talking about Hartley?"

"It's not that I'm looking to blame his office or anyone in particular. But just for the heck of it, why do you think the original transcription error happened? I heard Jane Carolli's take on it, but what do you think?"

"It sounds like it was nothing more than a lazy transcriptionist."

"Did you read the notes from Carolli's interview of the transcriptionist?"

"No."

"According to her, she couldn't read his notes and when she asked him he said, 'Just do your damn job.' She then looked at it again and couldn't figure it out so she asked Hartley a second time. And then the physician threatened her, 'If you can't do your job, I'll find someone who can.' Then, according to her, fear and frustration won out and she gave up and guessed."

"Why do we trust her version?"

"I know what you mean, especially after that meeting. How do we trust anyone's version of anything?"

"Wait a minute, Jack. That's going a little far, don't you think? Yes, Carolli is buried in work and maybe a little intimidated by Lang...I mean so am I— we all are—but that's probably a healthy survival instinct. I really don't know Hartley, but I do know, and I'm sure you'll agree, that everyone places physicians on a pedestal, as they should. Sometimes the only way to garner respect is through a little healthy fear."

"Ben, if that's true and we both realize that physicians are also leaders, then we're saying that a lot of the decisions and orders in this place are a result of people not knowing how to work together, plain and simple."

Ben agreed, "I guess that's accurate. Nobody around here is too comfortable with expressing opinions that will probably get shot down. But wait a second. First you're asking me about what the patients want, then whether physicians are leaders. I'm not sure where you're going with this."

"You're right," said Jack. "Let's break it down. Do you agree that physicians are perceived as leaders?"

"Yes."

"And most of the staff fear them?"

"Probably, but again, I'm sure there's more to it."

"What do you mean, Ben?"

"I don't know...I just wonder sometimes if the patients can see how dysfunctional we are."

"What do you mean by dysfunctional?"

"I didn't mean that; I guess I meant that we're not quite team players around here, and I can't help thinking that the patients see that."

"Do you think it's that blatant?"

"I'm not sure," answered Ben.

"Well, back in Billings, when I first started at the clinic, it seemed like everyone was working alone. When I asked a nurse about it, she told me that she no longer gave opinions anymore because nobody wanted them. She said it just felt safer to keep things to herself. Is that what's going on around here?"

"I'm sure that's one of our problems. Sounds about right."

"Do you think our, for lack of better words, unsafe environment contributed to Edie's problems?"

Ben hesitated. "Yes, obviously, after hearing the Hartley-transcriptionist conversation. I know everyone was doing the best they could, under the circumstances."

As Ben's last thought trailed off, he wasn't quite sure that he was hearing himself clearly. He had just defended behavior that helped kill one of his patients. He wasn't sure what point Jack was trying to get across.

Jack continued, "Did Dr. Lang execute his duties properly? Did he do his job?"

"I guess he did, but she's dead, isn't she?"

"Are you saying that it wasn't Lang's or Hartley's fault specifically, but the entire team—not one person—let her down?"

"I guess. Listen, Jack, I didn't even know we were a team. In fact, we're the furthest thing from it."

"What do you mean, Ben?"

"The patients probably assume we work like a team, but I know that's not the case, because it's always been every man for himself around here."

"Well, Ben, why do you think we don't work as teams around here?"

"I don't know. Maybe because it has always been that way...the nature of the beast."

"That doesn't mean it has to be that way moving forward."

Jack Martin just sat there and sipped his beer looking straight ahead.

Ben slugged down his beer and started to pull himself up off the barstool, his head swirling with ideas.

"I think I've had enough for tonight, Jack. You've given me a lot to think about. I'm going to head home to Mel."

TWENTY-THREE

The next morning, Dr. Jack Martin headed to the first of his three meetings with Melanie Swift, Jane Carolli, and Dr. Lang. Carolli told him he would be running the next NEI meeting, which originally revolved around him being responsible for building consensus for the new patient safety initiatives. But after the first debacle, Jack knew that initiatives weren't going to cut it. In fact, he knew that from the get-go.

As he headed to Melanie Swift's station he couldn't help thinking that Ben Waller was right—this did remind him of the hospital he just left, before they began to see things differently. The biggest difference was the scale of things. There were negative people at the clinic, but their reach and the scope of fear they generated didn't compare with how Dr. Lang's physician-protective, intimidating stance affected this entire organization. He didn't know if he'd ever "turn" Lang, but knew that as long as everyone in this hospital saw Jane Carolli so submerged with problems and not any more effective than the last guy, they would all follow Lang's lead. After all, they had for years. Leaders had come and gone, while Dr. Ethan Lang persevered.

Jack knew what needed to be done. If he was going to have a shot at changing things around here, it had to start with Jane Carolli.

As he turned the corner thinking about how to best approach Carolli, he ran smack dab into Mel.

"Whoa, Dr. Martin, when you said you wanted a few minutes to bounce a couple of things off of me, I didn't think you meant that literally."

He chuckled with embarrassment. "Very good, Ms. Swift."

"Call me Mel."

"Thanks, Mel, is there somewhere quiet we can escape to for a few minutes?"

"Follow me."

She led him into a small, empty sutures room where he sat at the patient's station while Mel took the stool she usually worked from.

He started, "I have a few specific questions about the NEI meeting. If you haven't heard, I'll be running the next one and I'm trying to get all my ducks in a row. Anyway, before I ask you a couple of things, why don't you give me your take on what happened?"

"That's pretty easy. I caved, which is a rarity for me, and Lang steamrolled his way through, as always. What really kills me is that Julie's going to get shafted for something she didn't do. In fact she was the only one in the operating room truly advocating for the patient. And she's paying for it. She's really crushed. Not to mention the fact that she still had a little of the idealism we all try to nurture and keep viable. But now, it's pretty much gone."

"I wouldn't be so sure that this is going to fall on Julie. I honestly believe something very good is going to come from this for all of us. Anyway, you said you caved, Mel. What really could you have done differently? If Jane Carolli didn't feel it was the right time to take on Ethan Lang, what would you have had to gain by taking him on then?"

"First of all, I don't think that Lang thinks he has a superior. As for Ms. Carolli, I am not sure. The jury is still out on her. She is relatively new, the first-ever woman to run this place, and she has the right to feel intimidated by Lang. Our last CEO was a good old boy down to his wingtips, but when he continued to disagree with Lang on one issue, Lang rallied the Medical Executive Committee to help initiate a no confidence vote on him, the next day."

"So, Mel, you really couldn't have done anything in the meeting, could you?"

"I could've stood up for Julie. I could've spoken truth to power, instead of acting like a craned-neck passerby at an accident."

"What about the outcome of the meeting, Mel? Do you think we can come up with some initiatives that really protect patients? Or is there something else we should be doing?"

"I'm sure we can. Whether or not we can get physicians like Lang and Hartley to abide by them is another story. But let's face it, this place isn't running short on initiatives. They seem to throw one at everything that needs a Band-Aid. I'm not sure what we should be doing. It goes a lot deeper than checklists. And Lord knows we have a ton of them already."

Jack didn't miss a beat, "You must have some ideas as to what this place needs."

"Sometimes, I think it's just too late for this place. Everyone is so afraid to speak up about anything; I see mishaps that should never happen, happen every day. After the news about Julie gets around, do you think any other nurse in this hospital will ever challenge a physician? When you work in a place where it's not perceived as safe to chime in, nothing will ever change."

Jack Martin saw the same resignation in Mel as he did in Ben Waller. Everyone obviously felt isolated.

"Mel, you don't seem like the kind of person who gives up that easily. Maybe we should be thinking about making this place feel safer for everyone to express their opinions instead of adding checklists?"

"Maybe, I don't know. Checklists aren't bad things. And if they're actually used, they do work. I have no idea how we would even begin to level the playing field around here. You're talking about changing the way people behave, how they relate to each other. Seems like a stretch. And generally, I don't throw in the towel, but it's like a constant battle against city hall around here. I only stay because I know it's no better elsewhere. As long as I have my patients, I guess it's all worth it. They give me what I need around here, not the hospital staff."

"Mel, other than great care, what do you give your patients?"

"I don't follow you."

"Let me ask it differently. What do you think your patients need the most from you?"

"A lot of things: quality care, timely responses to their problems, and maybe above all, someone who listens to them. Someone they can believe in."

"Someone who listens to them. Funny, isn't that what you want from the physicians around here?"

Mel was stopped in her tracks, looking puzzled. "I guess so, I've never thought of it that way."

Jack continued, "Well, your patients are pretty lucky to have you. And I believe you nailed it. When you're in a strange place, afraid for your life, nothing could be more comforting than having someone there to believe in. But what about the other people, the rest of your team? You can't be there all the time. And although it's great having your patients believe in you, what about when you're not there?"

Mel didn't really know how to answer. The way things were around here, she never thought of herself as being on a team, but she was sure that's what Dr. Martin was referring to.

Her silence spoke for her.

Jack broke the silence. "You just told me that your patients need to believe in you. They need to believe that you listen to them and respect what they have to say. Again, is that any different from how physicians, nurses, and everyone around here should deal with each other?"

"Sure, Dr. Martin, in a perfect world. There are a few of the nurses that I have pretty productive relationships with, and I'm trying to get Ben to be a more open communicator." Mel didn't plan on blurting out personal stuff, but it just came. This guy was pretty good at bringing things to the surface. "But when it comes to feeling 100 percent safe in approaching most everyone around here, it just doesn't work that way. If I want something done right, I can only count on me. Don't you see that?"

"It doesn't matter what I see. What about Edie? Do you think she felt like we were listening, like we were a team fighting for her?"

The smile left Mel's face. "It turned out that Edie couldn't count on any of us. And she needed to be able to count on all of us."

"Yes, we let her down. And it wasn't because one person screwed up. Mel, do you think there is anything you can do to change things around here?"

"You don't think I can possibly be responsible for how everyone else behaves?"

Jack hesitated. "Well, you're probably right. But what if—and I know it's a 'What if' with a capital W—what if you could affect how everyone else behaved?"

"Contrary to popular belief," said Mel, "I'm not wearing a Wonder Woman cape under these scrubs. Isn't that Carolli and the board's job?"

Jack continued. "Like you just said, Edie needed all of us to survive."

"I guess it's going to take all of us to change this place, if it's even possible. I mean, we have some really talented people here. They show up and work hard every day. But it's every man for himself. So if talent, getting results, and dedication aren't enough, what else is there? What can we do to change things?" said Mel.

"There are a lot of things we can do, and I'm going to introduce them during the next couple of NEI meetings. I can tell you this much, you have more power than you think. To make any substantive changes, it's going to start with one person who is willing to improve her relationship with one other person."

"Again, Doc, this sounds a little unreal to me. But I like the sound of it."

"I'm sure it does. I felt the same when I first started thinking about how to change things in Billings. But you have to be open to seeing things a little differently. You have to be open to changing behaviors that we've had drilled into us forever."

Jack Martin spent the next few minutes telling Mel the Viktor Frankl story, and when he finished, she sat for a few seconds and said, "Jeez, if only Lang..." And she let the unfinished thought just hang there.

Jack gave her a minute to process and then said, "Mel, thanks so much for your time. I'd really enjoy doing this again soon. I just have to get going."

"I don't know what to say, Dr. Martin. My head's spinning with all the stuff you talked about."

"You did just as much talking as I did. So let me add one more thing before I run. When you were talking earlier, you mentioned that you were trying to improve communicating with Ben."

"I didn't mean to say that."

"It's okay. In fact I'm glad that you did. Not that I want to pry into personal stuff or anything, but the same tools you can use to build a better relationship with Ben also work with your co-workers. Are you interested in talking about that?"

"Absolutely."

"Think about it." With that, Jack said good-bye and left.

Mel couldn't help wondering, *What planet was that guy from and what took so long for him to land in her hospital?*

TWENTY-FOUR

D r. Ethan Lang had grown tired of being surrounded by incompetents. It was ridiculous when you thought about it—physicians made up such a small percentage of the hospital staff, yet they were the only ones who really mattered.

He shrugged, thinking, *Even Simon Hartley is an idiot, but a great referrer. I haven't made up my mind about Ben Waller. Waller has played by the rules so far, but I can see his hesitancy flare up at times.* Lang knew Waller was being led astray by that fireball Swift, who had nothing but the wrong ideas and not nearly enough respect for physicians. He thought, *Don't these people have a clue who is responsible for this hospital's success? Without my guidance, this place probably would have slipped away into obscurity years ago. And even more importantly, whose ass is always on the line when things go wrong?*

His thoughts were interrupted mid-stream when Jack Martin knocked on the door and poked his head in.

Oh great, he thought, *I don't have any time to patronize this guy. I don't know why Carolli plucked him out of some backwater swamp somewhere, but he isn't going to last long here.*

"Martin, I really don't have time for you right now. Why don't you make an appointment with my girl and we can grab a cup of coffee next week?"

"Okay, Dr. Lang, it's just that after sitting through that meeting it became pretty clear that you're one of the leaders around here, and I thought that if I want to make some headway around here it would be great to have your help."

Lang took a second, thinking, *Is this guy brown-nosing me or does he possibly think he has a slim chance of getting me invested in whatever the heck he has planned? Either way, his naïveté won't serve him well here.*

"I appreciate that, Dr. Martin, but Jane Carolli really does a good job of keeping this place going. I'm just busy saving lives."

"You mean, you don't think of yourself as a leader here?"

"I'm just a surgeon."

"Come on, Doctor, I'm a physician. I know what the responsibilities are in a place like this."

"Then you should also know that they think we're responsible for everything that happens, whether it's our fault or not."

"You mean like Edie? Her death must have really gotten to you—I mean, knowing it was avoidable and all."

Lang didn't miss a beat. "Every death gets to me. Especially when somebody else's screw-up casts a shadow on my work. But as you know, we have to focus on the here and now in this business. There's nothing we can do about the past."

"So you think new pre-op initiatives will help prevent this from happening again?"

"I don't need the hospital to tell me how to prep for a surgery. My only mistake was trusting Hartley's notes, and they weren't even his fault."

"But isn't Dr. Hartley a leader here too?"

"What are you getting at, Martin?"

Jack mentally smoked his pipe a few seconds while Lang impatiently waited.

"You agree that we physicians are leaders too, right?"

"What the heck are you getting at?"

"Well, don't people at the top have to hold themselves accountable for their choices?"

"Of course."

"Then is Dr. Hartley responsible for the notes that came from his office?"

"You're not trying to blame this on him are you? If you attack one of my physicians, you won't last a week here."

"Whoa. I'm not blaming anyone, and this discussion is just between two physicians, no one else. I'm just trying to figure out the hierarchy around here."

Lang didn't know what to think. He knew that if Martin wasn't an MD, he would have already dismissed him. As annoying as this guy was, he couldn't help but respect a fellow fraternity member.

"Are we done for now, Martin? I need to get back to work."

"Do you mind if we follow up next week after the meeting?"

"Whatever."

TWENTY-FIVE

When Ben got the text from Mel asking him out on what seemed like a date, he felt pretty excited. He'd never been in such a romantic relationship, and she was really smart and easy to be around. She made him feel different than anyone ever had, maybe that's why he'd let her get so close to him. Even when she ticked him off, she always made sense. He just didn't know if he could completely close the deal with her until she accepted the hierarchy of their working relationship. She really believed that all things were equal at the hospital. She talked to physicians like they were working for her.

He wasn't sure how things would work out when he headed out to meet her for a meal at the Brooklyn on Second Avenue. A lot of people went there for the steaks, but Ben loved their oyster selection, and hopefully tonight he'd utilize their power in every way possible.

It was so rare for him to be going out to dinner at the dinner hour, so the amount of people waiting for seats caught him off guard. Then he saw Mel pop up out of one of the captain's chairs at the dining bar, facing the line cooks. He knew she'd force him to talk more about work than he wanted, but maybe the best way to get her down from her soapbox quickly was to nod like a bobblehead and just let her vent.

When he approached the chair, she grabbed him and gave him a kiss that about straightened his hair. What the hell?

"What did I do to deserve that, Mel?"

"Well, we are living together aren't we? And to be honest, I've missed spending time with you outside of the hospital."

"Me too, Mel. I just thought you'd be pretty upset after that meeting."

"And you still came to dinner. There's hope for you yet, Dr. Waller."

"Well go ahead then, give me your worst."

"If you had asked me to do that this morning, Ben, I would have been on you like white on rice, but my meeting with Jack Martin got me thinking."

"Yes, he's a pretty interesting guy," said Ben. "When we had a beer together we talked about listening to our patients and creating a kind of environment where people feel safe to say anything they want, and then he asked me who I felt free to talk with about anything."

"So what did you say?" asked Mel.

"I said some of my colleagues, but that's about as far as I got. He was skirting around the need for all of us to feel safe about speaking up, which you know is not the case around Angels."

Ben asked, "What about you, Mel? Who do you feel safe talking with?"

"I told him I communicate better with you than anyone else, but, and I'm sorry Ben, you listen to me, but you don't always respect what I'm saying."

"What does that mean?"

"It means that you sometimes minimize what I say because I'm not an all-knowing, all-powerful physician like you. But, Ben, I would never have let you into my life or moved in with you if I didn't feel safe with you. It's just that if this is the real deal, I need to know that you respect what I have to say, even if I didn't go to medical school. If this is going to be a long-term thing, then we have to be real partners—fifty-fifty. I need to know that my opinion matters."

"I do value your opinion, Mel, it's just that this is how I've always been. There are physicians and then there are nurses. No matter what happens to a patient, the physician has to make the big decisions and is held the most accountable. I'm trying not to carry that into our personal life. In fact, I'm not sure I do all that much. Look, we were talking about work, and I was a little taken aback when I heard you were sharing our personal stuff with a perfect stranger."

"Ben, he's no longer a stranger. Maybe a little strange, but he is a good guy, and I'm learning a lot from him."

"Fine, I just wish you would keep our personal stuff separate from work stuff."

"I just can't help but see parallels. I'm not trying to embarrass you or anything. It's just that the way Dr. Martin talks about wanting us all to work together as a team, is kind of the way I'd like to see us work together."

She paused for a second to let that sink in.

"Ben, on the work front, right before we finished, he was complimenting me about my dedication, but then briefly mentioned something about what happens when I'm not around. He said something about the rest of my team and how they show up."

Glad to be back on the work front, Ben said, "Your team...what team...this guy really is clueless."

"I don't think so. After I told him that I can't be responsible for how everyone else shows up, he asked me, 'What if you could affect how everyone else shows up?' and I didn't know how to reply. I've been trying to go over the whole Edie incident in my head and I realized that if I could wave my magic wand and change just one tiny behavior, she would be alive today."

Ben didn't know where she was going with this. It might be out of the realm of reality, but she wasn't putting a target on his back, he thought, so he might as well go with the flow.

"What would that be, Mel?"

"You ever hear of Viktor Frankl, Ben?"

"Nope."

"I learned about him from Jack."

And she proceeded to tell Ben the story.

"I've got to agree, Mel, he sounds pretty impressive, but what does this have to do with waving your magic wand?"

"Don't you get it, Ben? In the midst of insanity, this guy had the wherewithal, the focus to, I don't know, freeze everything around him in a concentration camp long enough to think rationally about his responses to things. He realized that how he responded to the terror was the only thing they couldn't take away from him. If I could've waved my wand and gotten Lang to stop for a second and have a 'Frankl moment' when Julie asked him to check out the scan, he would've spent five seconds analyzing his response to find out the discrepancy with the lobes, and Edie would be alive today."

Ben was about to respond when the waiter came with Mel's rib eye and his Kumamoto oysters. He would rather have just eaten, drunk a boatload of wine, and taken her back home, but she was not about to let things lie.

After the waiter left Ben said, "That would've been great, Mel, but let's get real here. Dr. Martin's ideas sound wonderful if you like fiction. But you don't have a magic wand, and what are we supposed to do with this information? Me aside, you're never going to get Lang to listen to a nurse. He might be overly arrogant, but he does focus on his work and gets the job done. We are all too busy just doing our jobs; we can't be responsible for how others show up. It sounds a little too far-fetched for me."

"I agree, Ben, it sounds kind of weird, but I think Jack has something more up his sleeve. And if I just accept that things can never get any better around here, I might as well pack it in now. I know I do my best for my patients, but what happens once I am gone? The other nurses are taking their own approach, which has to contribute to a patient feeling a little unsettled. And who knows how many times each of us ask our patients the same things because we're not communicating with each other enough?"

"Look, Mel, we're here to get them better. If you start thinking that you're responsible for anything else, you're just setting yourself up for a letdown."

"At least you're consistent, Ben. Consistently cynical."

"Mel, can we just let this go for the night and go home? I'm sure I can make you forget about everything for a while."

"Fine, Ben, but whether at work or at home, this isn't just going away."

And then she took a big bite of steak and chewed and smiled. Ben hoped it was the thought of the evening ahead of them, but it was probably about the steak.

TWENTY-SIX

When her secretary's line buzzed, Jane Carolli was thinking about five things at once. She had read somewhere that the once-hip idea of multi-tasking wasn't so hip after all. In her case, she knew that she would do a better job if she did one thing at a time. Then she looked at her list. How could she possibly do one thing at a time and ever get through this mess?

When her secretary announced Dr. Jack Martin was there, her mind suddenly flooded with Lang, the patient Edie, and all the litigation. She really needed his help.

"Send him in."

"Hi, Jack, have a seat."

"Thanks, Jane, how are you doing? We really haven't had much time to talk since I arrived."

"I know, and to be quite honest, I really need your help. I have people pulling at me from every which way and I'm growing a little tired of the same juggling act day after day."

"Where do you want to start?"

"I was hoping that you would tell me. I definitely want to know how you were going to handle the NEI follow-up, and more specifically, how you were going to deal with Dr. Lang."

After seeing Lang ramrod the meeting, Jack knew a lot of Jane's frustrations began with him. At least that's probably how she saw it.

"Before we go down that road, Jane, I've got to tell you that pacifying Lang is just dealing with a symptom of the bigger challenges we have here."

"Let me interrupt, Jack. I know where you're going with this, and I brought you here because of what you did in Billings, but right now, I have to deal with an immense amount of problems and you'll have to wait for a more opportune time to move forward with our big-picture agenda. Right now, I need to be able to not focus on Lang so I can focus on everything else that's going on around here."

"Then let me take out a gun and shoot you in the foot right now so you can get used to limping though your days. You told me you wanted straight talk from me, right?"

"Yes, but..."

"No, Jane, I came here to help you really make some concrete changes, and you know as well as I do, if we wait for a good time to start anew, we never will. Do you really foresee a time when you won't be as busy as you are now?"

"No, but..."

Cutting her off again, he said, "Good. Remember when we talked about the staff in Billings and differentiated between repeatedly dealing with symptoms versus finding a cure for our root cause problems?"

"Yes."

"That we accomplished all those changes without adding new initiatives to the mix—you know, no extra work?"

Again, he didn't give her time to answer.

"Jane, I promise I'll shut up in a minute and get to your concerns, but I need to validate that we are still on the same page, because if you recall, the key to moving and curing the problems we have at Angels depends on your buy-in first. And regardless of what kind of grip you feel Lang has on this hospital, you are the top dog."

Well this guy doesn't mess around, does he? She knew he was pretty proactive and fearless, but this was the first she'd seen it since their initial drink at the convention. *Did he really just tell her that she perceives herself as being under Lang's thumb?* She knew she was running Angels; Lang just kept getting in her way and slowing her down.

"Okay, Dr. Martin. How do you think we should proceed here?"

Dr. Jack Martin paused for a second while he reminded himself that although the size of this place was a little intimidating, he was sure he knew what Angels needed, and he knew how to help.

After regaining his confidence, he realized that no matter how big this place was, Jane Carolli was just one person and it all begins with one-to-one relationships. And that's how he had to approach things—one person at a time, then small groups, and then the small groups going viral.

"Pretty soon, Jane, I'll need to start getting some of your key medical staff to realize that things can change around here. I need to get the light bulbs to go on in their heads. I know that half or more of what I tell them will land on deaf ears. But if I can get them to connect some dots internally, we'll be on our way. Secondly, I need you to work with me to begin leading differently. Look, I know you know you're the boss. And although Lang has built a protective wall around most of the physicians, that doesn't mean that anyone likes it, or him, for that matter. He offers protection and leverages fear to gain cooperation. I'd be willing to bet that most everyone here would love the opportunity to abandon his ship if they didn't think they were risking career suicide by doing so. They just haven't seen any other options."

"Although what you're saying makes sense, you just got here. I've been walking on pins and needles for the last year. I haven't been able to make any positive changes whatsoever, and as much as I would like to believe you, I'm not feeling very hopeful right now."

"Jane, do you remember what impressed you about what we accomplished in Billings?"

Jane thought back to her conversation with Jack's last boss, Bill Stone. Normally, CEOs aren't thrilled when you cull one of their physicians, and they won't give you the time of day, but he was resigned to the fact that Jack was moving on regardless. So surprisingly, he sang Jack's praises over three different calls. That alone told her volumes about the cultural shift that had taken place.

"Well, Bill Stone said that part of it was intangible. The entire hospital and clinic eventually gained a relaxed feeling he'd never experienced before. On the tangible side, he said his staff meetings weren't really run by any one person, but more was accomplished in forty-five minutes than in ten of his 'old' meetings. The change seemed most apparent when everyone sat down and worked as teams, instead of physicians only working with fellow physicians and nurses only working with nurses. Nurses, physicians, managers...they were all contributing without stepping all over what the others were saying. He said to me that he thought (at the time) that it was sad that this had to sound remarkable and wasn't commonplace. Everyone actually listened to the other's perspective, realizing that they needed it to chart their own most effective course."

"Well don't you think that's how it should be, Jane?"

"I never really thought about it before. I mean, if you were to tell me that physicians would be genuinely listening to nurses' ideas...please, Jack, that alone made me wonder what the hell they put in the coffee. It sounded like a Stepford Hospital."

"And that doesn't sound good to you?"

"Jack, I like what you all accomplished in Billings, or you wouldn't be here. But I am not convinced yet that we can duplicate it. And I'd just love to get Lang to have less influence around here. I don't care if he disagrees with everything we're trying to do—I just want him to keep his mouth shut."

"You need to stop thinking in terms of getting rid of or influencing Lang, and instead, begin to focus on making positive behavioral changes around here. If we can just tweak this culture a bit, Lang will be the one having to make decisions about his future here, not you."

He continued, "Jane, everything you heard about Billings was a result of people showing up willing to listen and learn. And that's all I'm asking of you now."

"Of course I'm on the same page as you, Jack, remember, I'm the one who asked you here. This is just such a new way of thinking, and it takes a little time to get used to it."

"I know. And we're going to have to ask the same of everyone in this organization eventually. But it begins with you. Because, believe it or not, however you show up every day affects how everyone else shows up...just like a teacher sets the tone of a classroom and the principal sets the tone of the school."

Jane Carolli didn't know what to say. She saw her cynicism rear its ugly head, and maybe even felt a little sorry for herself. She immediately thought, *Whoa, Jane, you knew this wasn't going to happen overnight. You trust yourself and this guy, so keep your eyes on the ball.*

"Okay, Jack, I'll listen. Where do we go from here?"

"Jane, before we get deeper into this, let's talk for a second about how you see yourself as a leader."

"What do you mean?"

"Well, everything we're doing together right now is only possible because I'm approaching my relationship with you as a coach."

"I know, Jack, you just mentioned coaching when we were talking about the physicians...I get it."

He continued, "I know, but I want to explore it a little bit further. I need you to see yourself as a coach too. Humor me."

She urged him, "Go on."

"What do you think when I say your role as a coach is the foundation for how you lead?"

"Jack, you're saying that coaching is the most important thing I can do?"

"Yes, Jane, and if we all want to truly be patient-centered...to build patient-centered relationships, we have to be coaches, and teach others to do the same. In Billings, things changed when my boss started coaching his leadership team, and eventually his medical staff. Listen, Jane, this is how it begins. We're about to make a pact to improve our relationship, and even though you're my boss and I report to you, we're moving into this new area as peers. I'm coaching you through it while modeling how to operate as a coach."

Jane sat for a second before saying, "So you're saying that just as we can teach each other how to improve our relationship, we need to teach each other to be coaches."

"You got it."

"Okay, Jack, then let's get on with this relationship-building exercise of yours."

"Okay, but before we begin making promises to each other, and penciling out an agreement, we should make sure we're on the same page as far as where we perceive we're at now, and where we want to get to."

"I'm not sure I follow."

"Let's talk about what drives us crazy now, and what the best-case scenario looks like."

"What drives me crazy? I hope you have a lot of paper."

"Go for it."

Jack pulled out a notepad while Jane stared seemingly at nothing and then said, "Almost everyone is all talk and very little action. Sure, they do their jobs, but not a day goes by where problems that they should've handled themselves find their way up the ladder to my desk. I seem to be picking up all the slack around here. If I could only get people to work together a little,

I probably wouldn't be managing so much of their stuff."

"Keep going."

"Well, no matter how much I try to set an example, as far as getting most people to be proactive and go beyond what their job requires, I get nothing. Modeling the right behaviors has had no impact around here. Again, I'm consistently dealing with problems they should've handled themselves. Is it too much to ask that someone other than myself solves problems around here?"

"Of course not...is that it?"

"Here's a few off the top of my head. First, I am sick and tired of having such low expectations. And secondly, I see the same bad behaviors, or bad habits, continually repeated. And it seems like everybody is fine with the status quo."

"Okay, that's enough to start with. Over the next few days, keep a pad on your desk and write down anything else that crosses your mind, and we'll sift through them and whittle them down."

"Now comes the fun part. How would you like this place to look and operate if you had it your way?"

Jane thought about it for a minute. "My physicians are really smart, Jack. They're as technically proficient as any I've worked with. And no matter how bad some of their behaviors and attitudes are, they all have a sense of dedication that's palpable. Most of the time they get excellent clinical results. But that's not always enough."

"Jane, you seem to be talking about individuals who are good at their jobs. In fact, what you just shared mirrors the criteria used for hiring physicians."

"Yes, that sounds about right. So why are we so screwed up around here?"

"Well, you're talking about individual people doing their jobs. What about the bigger picture. How do they fit in here? What part do they play in the big picture?"

"I'm not sure what you mean."

"Jane, we're trained to look at people and judge them by how well they do their jobs, but it's much bigger than that."

"Jack, you keep alluding to playing our parts, our roles. What specifically do you mean?"

"It's just that doing your job, no matter how well, isn't enough. If our physicians and nurses all do their jobs well, but still don't communicate, the patient will still suffer negative consequences. When they realize that what they do affects everyone, both negatively and positively, then we can open the door toward effectively working together, and also give the patient the peace of mind knowing that everyone is on the same page concerning their case."

"That makes sense, but it seems a long way off when all I can see is a staff set in their ways and not about to change."

"Well you already mentioned that they're pretty unresponsive to you, and they all have individual bad habits that you can't seem to influence. What if you could break some of those habits? What end results would you like to see?"

"If I could get them to listen to each other without judging, and set their egos aside long enough to have honest conversations, they could actually solve some problems together. Why should that sound like such a foreign concept, Jack, having teams working together? That's what you guys eventually had in Billings. The staff meetings Bill Stone talked about weren't a result of some rocket science creation, you guys just learned to respect each other enough to work as an effective team."

"And that's doable, Jane. Not overnight, or next week, but it's definitely doable, and I know that from personal experience. I'll write these notes up, and some things that I could improve on for you too, and the next time we meet, we'll figure out what both of us have to agree to, to make this happen between us. Again, this is the first step in this entire process. We can't just tell everyone about it—we have to teach them how it's done by changing the way they show up."

"I wish we could have started this a year ago, Jack."

"We have to take baby steps. It's the only way it will work."

"Is this what you're planning to introduce in the NEI meeting?"

"Yes, but very slowly. I think we'll need at least two more NEIs to introduce some of this."

"Wow," said Jane, "this ought to be interesting."

TWENTY-SEVEN

en was on an espresso mission. His office coffee wasn't cutting it after only a couple of hours of sleep. At home, he couldn't get enough of Mel. He still couldn't get her around to his way of thinking at work, but there would be time for that.

As he turned the corner toward the espresso stand, he caught a glimpse of Jack Martin and quickly looked down at the ground, hoping to avoid him.

"Ben, I was just thinking of you."

Of course you were, thought Ben, *now that Mel let you into our personal lives.*

"Dr. Martin, how are you this fine morning?"

"Thanks for asking. Great. And I'll be even better if I can get this next NEI meeting scheduled."

"Just get some times over to my office and Betty will get you on the calendar."

"Thanks, it's just that I don't want to put together a repeat of the last meeting. I was hoping to get the groundwork developed with some clear-cut goals before we get into the room again. And it would really help if you and Ms. Swift could meet with me first, to gather a consensus before we face the rest of the participants."

Ben knew Jack was focused on Lang and possibly Carolli. Jack was smart enough to understand that Lang really affected the tone here and that if he couldn't get him onboard, he'd have to figure out a plan to render him a non-factor. And he wouldn't get him onboard. He already knew not to bother with the other two physicians involved. They had clearly demonstrated their loyalties at the last meeting and that wouldn't change. The last few times Ben had talked with Hartley, all he talked about was retiring very soon and how he was going to spend a lot of time sailing up near his San Juan home on Lopez Island.

"I don't know how much value I could provide, Jack. Remember, I was Edie's physician, but I wasn't in the operating room."

"But you found out what really happened from Ms. Swift?"

Ben leaned back on his heels, thinking, *Now he's going try to nail me. Now his agenda's becoming clear.*

"Yes, she told me Julie's story."

"I know you weren't there and your knowledge is secondhand, but I don't want to meet with you guys to talk about blame or any incident specifics anyway. I want to figure out the underlying causes of what happened and make sure we don't make the same mistakes again."

"How are you going to do that?"

"I have an idea, but I need your input, your help."

And the other shoe falls, thought Ben. *Now this guy wants me to do his job for him.*

"I don't know what I can do for you. Mel might have some ideas on a pre-op checklist."

"That's just it. Honestly, do you think building the world's best checklist is going to prevent this from happening again?"

"Checklists can be very effective, but honestly, no."

"Me neither. But I do know from past experience that dealing directly with the underlying causes of our problems is paramount, and all I want to do is talk about that and see if it makes sense to you two. I'm also currently working to build consensus with Jane Carolli. I figure if we all show up to the next meeting on the same page, Lang and the rest may just have to listen."

"You're assuming he's going to show up at all."

"True. Worst case scenario, we leave him behind."

Ben wasn't exactly sure where Jack was going with this, but he was clueless if he thought he could take on Lang. *He's my bread and butter,* thought Ben, *no matter what a jerk he is.*

"This sounds an awful lot like a set-up to a confrontation, Jack, and I don't want any part of that."

"You're reading me wrong, Ben. I don't want anyone to confront anyone. I just want to have a conversation. Listen, we had some of the same problems in Billings that we have here. We went about things a little bit differently than the norm, and we created some great outcomes. I'd just like to share some of that with you guys and see where it goes. Look, let's just you and Mel and I sit down for a couple of beers and have a conversation—I'm buying. I'm not asking you to do any extra work or for that matter, do anything."

Ben felt like he was having a one-on-one with a pit bull. And Jack wasn't about to take his teeth out of him until he got what he wanted. He might as well get it over with.

"Fine, Jack, figure something out with Mel and get me the info. But I'm not promising you any positive outcomes."

TWENTY-EIGHT

Mel started her Sunday morning like most, a quick first look at her charges' charts beginning with Mrs. Morton, a seventy-five-year-old with a long history of inflammatory bowel disease and associated abscesses...she had had twenty surgeries, but the abscesses continued to come back. And she was scheduled for another surgery tomorrow.

Mel poked her head in Mrs. Morton's room, immediately noticing she was in pain, perspiring heavily, and guarding her abdomen when she shifted herself around on the bed.

She couldn't understand why Peg Lawton, the night nurse, hadn't looked into upping her pain medications. Peg came up from behind her, purse in hand, heading for the door.

"Hi, Peg, you have a second before you go?"

"What, Mel, everything on the floor is copacetic and I'm beat and out the door. The charts are caught up. Can we visit tomorrow?"

"Just a quick question about Mrs. Morton here. She seems to be in pretty severe pain—have you checked with Dr. Salzan about upping her meds?"

She defensively snapped back, "Do you think I'm incapable of doing my job?"

"Whoa, slow down, Peg, I'm just looking out for a patient here. Maybe the pain just started, I don't know, I just want to get her some relief. I am not attacking you."

"She doesn't need any more medication. She only complained a little and I see no reason to bother the physician when she'll have the problem taken care of first thing tomorrow morning."

"Why should she suffer until then?"

As soon as she said it, Mel realized that she could have been more diplomatic in her approach, even if she was right. This idea of taking a few seconds before responding would have come in handy, but it was going to take some practice.

"Look, she has a long history of narcotic use and I don't want to support what seems to be a drug problem. Just do what you want; you're the boss and the one here now. Just as I'll do what I want to do when I'm here."

"Peg, why does this have to be about what we want? Shouldn't it be about what Mrs. Morton needs? Yes, she has been prescribed pain medications for years, but she seems to really need them right now."

"Get off your frickin' high horse, Mel. I've been doing this for longer than you have and I don't need you or anyone telling me what the hell to do. You're the manager, do what you want." She turned and left.

Mel immediately went in to talk with Mary Morton. She determined that her pain was indeed real, and she headed for the nurses' station to call Dr. Salzan's service for permission to up her meds.

She felt a presence behind her and swiveled around just as Dr. Jack Martin said, "Good morning, Ms. Swift. I was wondering if you had a second?"

A little irritated, she semi-hissed, "Just a second, Dr. Martin, I've got a pretty full plate right now."

Jack backpedaled, saying, "Sorry. I didn't mean to gum up the works; I just wanted to set up a time to visit with you and Ben together over a couple of beers."

Realizing that her claws had involuntarily sprung, she calmed herself, saying, "Sorry, Doc, but I'm just getting pretty sick and tired of using half of my energy fighting other nurses over patient care. But I shouldn't be bitching to you. Sorry."

"No problem, that's what I'm here for. So are you and Ben free tonight after work?"

"I am, but I'll have to check with Ben. He's not real thrilled about talking over any of this stuff. I probably shouldn't say this, but he's under the misguided notion that other than the potential lawsuit, things are status quo around here. I'm having a hard time getting him to see that no matter how good of a surgeon his protector Dr. Lang is, he has quite a lot of negative impact around here too."

"It's pretty clear that Lang has a pretty strong influence over most everyone around here."

"But not you, Dr. Martin?"

"Although I respect who he is, his experience, and what he means to this hospital, one person's expertise shouldn't trump the combined efforts of everyone else, no matter how gifted he is. It just doesn't make any sense. But we can talk about that later. Will you guys be free to meet me?"

"Sure," she answered, "but before you go, I've been thinking about what we talked about, and your offer to talk about what's going on here is tied to what's going on in my personal relationship with Ben. If you have a few minutes now, I just need to take care of one thing."

"Sure."

Mel reached Dr. Salzan, got approval, and took the pain meds to Mrs. Morton. While Mel led Jack to a vacant suture room she thought about how out of character it was for her to talk to anyone, much less an almost–stranger, about anything personal. But this guy had some kind of mojo working for him that made him seem approachable and easy to talk to. She knew Ben wouldn't like her doing this, but she had to go with her gut.

"So tell me, Dr. Martin...Jack, about the advantages of being a little bit more deliberate when I speak."

Jack added, "Creating that space to think before you respond."

"Yes, thanks. I'm trying to think about creating that space and I'd love to know more. I know we only have a few minutes."

"Well, Mel, before I talk about it on a personal level, let's bring into context what these NEI meetings are supposed to do."

"You mean Edie?" sighed Mel.

"Yes, Edie. Look at what happened when we didn't create space in the OR. The consequences of rushing to judgment without taking the time to listen and think...they can be deadly."

Mel responded, "Is it really that simple? I mean, if Lang had paused five seconds, thought, and looked at the scan, Edie would probably be alive. This pause thing is better than any checklist. It's a built-in, always-there checklist."

"Right, Mel, but don't be too hasty to put it all on Dr. Lang. He, like the rest of us, is a victim of what we've been taught and the current environment we work in. Things have to change at a much bigger level."

Looking a little exasperated at the scope of what Jack had just said, Mel moved on, "So how did you get going on all this, Jack?"

"Well, I may seem to have it together. But I'm constantly checking myself to make sure I hold myself accountable first, and then it becomes possible to help others do the same."

"What do you mean? You seem to already have it together."

"Seem is the key word, Mel. Granted, I have had success in the past, but I still struggle just like you do. We're all growing. And I've found that the best thing I can do to feel good about myself is to truly hold myself accountable. Whether it's at work, picking up after myself at home, or any personal goals, I have to be responsible for my actions, whether good or bad. I know this sounds pretty basic and simple, but that's because we hear it a lot. Living it is a different story."

"Keep going, Jack."

"Through living that way, I've become more honest with myself and I can more consistently count on myself to do the right thing, like listening to others and not discounting anyone. I'm not afraid to say what's on my mind because I have confidence in my decisions, because I listen and learn before I make up my mind...which is not to say that I don't still make mistakes. And then I started to realize how powerful it would be if everyone thought this way. Hopefully, you don't think that it's too egotistical and presumptuous to say that."

"Not at all. I can see how that's applicable at work. Most of my nurses don't share much, because they're shot down so often, before they even open their mouths."

Jack added, "I'm sure. And in your personal life, maybe thinking this way would help your communication with Ben improve. You know, we physicians are trained to be accountable or responsible to our patients, but not to each other or our staff."

"So what do I do with this information?"

"Well, Mel, I'm not a therapist, but I do believe that nothing changes overnight. I expect things could improve here, and with you and Ben, but it's going to come from baby steps, one relationship at a time, then small groups, and so on."

Mel sat thinking how everything made sense, but she was hoping for a roadmap or some quick-fix directions. She sure had a lot to think about.

"Mel, we can talk about this again, but I want you to know that over the next few weeks, I'm going to share all of this and a lot more with Ben and the others in the NEI group. Jane Carolli and I are working on it already. That's why she brought me here in the first place. When you see how things start coming together at work, you'll know what to do at home. Just be patient and try to re-evaluate your own mindset. Take it one step at a time."

As Mel got up to leave the suture room, her head was filled with new ideas and a newfound respect for Dr. Jack Martin and Jane Carolli. She couldn't help thinking, *I guess I underestimated her from the start.*

TWENTY-NINE

Normally Ben loved to meet Mel for a drink after work. Sometimes they played the strangers game of meeting in a bar while pretending not to know each other. They'd get a little tipsy and he'd sweep her off her feet and take her home. But that wasn't going to happen with Jack Martin riding shotgun.

Neither of them had eaten, and Mel was dying for a roasted chicken at Le Pichet, a little French bistro on First Avenue that made you feel like the Eiffel Tower sat waiting down the street.

Jack and Mel already had a table and were munching on some cheese and baguettes when Ben gave Mel a kiss on the cheek. "Bonjour, mon ami."

"I think you mean 'Bonsoir,' Ben, but I love it when you speak French to me, darling," Mel said in her best Morticia Addams.

"Hey, Ben," Jack added, "thanks so much for coming."

Yeah sure, he said to himself...*first let's get the most important stuff out of the way.* "Mel, did you get the chicken order in?"

"I did."

"Great. Okay, Jack, go ahead, we might as well dive into this stuff before the food comes."

"Well, the next meeting is scheduled in three days and I wanted to make sure that something productive comes out of it. I have two goals in mind. First, I need to follow procedure and dig a little deeper into what exactly went wrong to make sure we build in valid, implementable safeguards, and not just another checklist. Second, and most importantly, I want to look at how the culture around here made it possible for this to happen in the first place and begin talking about what we can do about it."

Ben couldn't help himself. "Is that all? In all candor, Jack, I think we know how this happened. We know that a nurse—sorry Mel—and a transcription-ist screwed up."

Mel almost exploded. "Ben, are you really going to keep going down that road? Are you in complete denial? I told you that Julie did nothing wrong and the screwup started with Hartley and was carried through by Lang."

"Look, Mel, I'll say this one last time. Dr. Lang is a great surgeon and had no reason to not believe in the chart. And you should remember that the nice condo we have, the Porsche, and my diminishing loan balances are all made possible because of Dr. Lang plugging me into his network."

While Jack Martin sat taking it all in, Mel just about lost it.

"You think Lang is the key to your having a successful career? You are so wrong. It's you Ben. You built your practice. Lang had his buddies send referrals your way, but you gave good care and grew a dedicated patient base on your own, because of how you treated them. You don't need Lang or any of his buddies to be successful."

"Sorry, Mel, I appreciate that, but I still think it's a little naïve."

Before Mel could answer Jack Martin broke in. "Whoa, wait a second, you two. Think about what you're arguing about. It seems that all we ever talk about is how our colleagues are determining what happens around here, especially Dr. Lang."

Great, thought Ben, *now I'm being tag-teamed.*

"Listen, Jack and Mel, yes Ethan Lang can be abrasive and he treats people with disrespect sometimes. But he's unselfishly taken the time to truly kick-start my career."

Mel was quietly seething. "At no benefit to himself, Ben?"

"I get it," Jack added. "Lang really influences a lot of what goes on around here. But only if you keep letting him."

Ben really wanted to straighten this guy out.

"This isn't about letting him. I need him," said Ben, not believing he had just said that. Since when did he depend on anyone that much?

He thought Mel was going to grab that one and really run with it when she came back calmly. "Do you really need him, Ben?"

He didn't know how to respond.

"Ben, Mel, do you remember the first thing I asked both of you?"

"Kind of," Mel answered. "Something about what our patients want. But what does this have to do with Ben and Dr. Lang?"

"I love it when I'm in the room and talked about in the third person."

"Oh come on Ben, grow up."

"Okay, hold on," said Jack. "You guys can duke it out later, if that's what you really want to do. Let me answer the question. When you focus your time and energy on Lang, or for that matter on other nurses, Mel, you're letting personality conflicts partially determine what and how you do things. What about the patient?"

"Come on, Jack," said Ben. "When are you going to stop being a broken record?"

Mel pounced, "Are you kidding, Ben? You're the broken record around here. Have you ever listened to yourself talk about how superior you physicians, especially Lang, are? You're so far above the rest of us and responsible for everything that's right around here?"

"Wait a second," said Jack, "do you see how easy it is to fall into the blame trap around here? The reason I keep bringing up the patient is because no matter how much we all got into this business to help people, and no matter how much we still feel that commitment, we're not basing what we do on what the patient needs. Are either of you capable of stepping outside of yourselves and your problems with your co-workers for a minute to see that?"

Not knowing how to respond, Ben was glad that the chicken arrived and they all began to eat, focusing their energy on the birds.

But Ben couldn't help but think, *Is that what Mel really thinks of me? I'm a broken record that needs to grow up? If she's right, then the only way things can work out between her and me is for me to distance myself from Lang, which will happen on its own if I decide to work directly for the hospital. Does she realize that I have everything to lose?*

Jack Martin broke Ben's thoughts and the almost continuous stream of chewing and swallowing by saying, "I know I just arrived here. I realize that where I came from is a different place entirely, with different personalities, and unique problems. But I also see vivid commonalities."

He continued. "There are Langs everywhere. Every hospital in this country is dealing with initiatives, overload, and a boatload of distinct personalities that have a huge effect on how we do things. I'm just saying that things need to change if we are to best serve our patients. And there is a way to change it. A way to put the patient in the center of everything we do. But only if you're open to it."

Ben didn't know why he took the bait, but he said, "Okay, Jack, things can change around here. I'll bite. What do we do? What's the magic bullet look like?"

"That all depends on you two, Lang, Carolli, and the rest of your medical staff. And it begins with how you come into the NEI meeting. If you come in with the goal of deflecting blame or on a mission of self-preservation, things will never change. But if you come to the meeting with your mind open to looking at what happened clinically and relationally, leaving behind the blame game, we might just end up focusing on how this won't ever happen again. And that's the first step toward doing what's best for our patients."

Jack gave them a second to take it in and continued. "Yes, we are going to go over the process of what led to the Edie disaster. But please, please try to add only what you know to be factual. If we clinically dissect things with the knowledge that nobody is getting thrown under the bus, that nobody is there to take advantage of anyone else, we have a chance of really clarifying the reasons for the breakdowns and why they occurred in the first place."

Mel quickly added, "You're never going to get Ethan Lang to do that."

Ben couldn't disagree. "If he even shows up."

THIRTY

Jack Martin spent the next morning camped out at Dr. Ethan Lang's office door to intercept him before the day swallowed him alive. He realized that Lang might not cooperate and pull others down around him, but, as he mentioned to Ben and Melanie, his experience in Billings had its share of Langs.

Most of them eventually came along for the ride and bought in. A few left. Some of the old dogs were capable of new tricks, others were not. If he had to bet now, he'd bet against Lang, but that kind of thinking left him feeling ineffectual, causing him to internally snap to attention and put those negative thoughts away.

Lang showed up in his camel hair overcoat, looking like a founding member of the gentry class.

"Dr. Lang, I really need your help for just a minute. I promise not to keep you long, but I've grown to realize that I'm not going to get much done around here without your help."

Not knowing if Martin was a complete brown-nose, he took the bait and ushered Martin into his office. "I only have five minutes, Martin. Make it quick."

Jack didn't bother sitting. "Dr. Lang, tomorrow is the second NEI meeting and I'll be running it."

"Well, have fun without me."

"That's the problem. I can't really get anything done without you. I know that the transcriptionist made the error..."

"And don't forget about that nurse."

"Yes, I know about what she says she did. But I'm not looking to assign blame. And I know as well as you do that a new checklist is a semi-waste of time if it doesn't have any teeth to it. You see, this is a chance to build a safeguard into the system based on how physicians think nurses and others need to adapt behaviorally to ensure this kind of thing doesn't happen again."

"So what do you want from me?"

"I want to use your knowledge and experience to focus the document where it needs to focus. I need to leverage the power of leadership you've earned here and try to come up with something substantive. And after that, we need to focus on the fundamental reason this kind of thing can happen in the first place, and make sure it doesn't happen again."

"I have no idea where to begin helping you and no time or desire to give it much thought. Although it would be good if we can avoid a repeat of what happened, if only to keep us from having redundant NEI meetings. And of course I feel bad for that poor girl..."

"Edie...yes, well don't worry about what we need to do; I have an idea of where to start. I just need your help. We all just need you to at least appear to lead the way."

"How long will this thing last?"

"No more than thirty minutes. And if it goes longer, you can just leave. As long as we all feel your influence and support going in."

"Fine. Thirty minutes."

He then opened up his appointment book and dismissed the new vice president for Medical Affairs without uttering another word.

THIRTY-ONE

On the morning of the second NEI meeting, Dr. Jack Martin did patient rounds, even though he didn't have any patients.

At his previous post he was tasked with trying to improve patient safety in an organization plagued by an unengaged medical staff. He hadn't a clue where to begin. One morning, out of frustration and the need to get out of his chair, he started walking the hospital floors.

As he slowly sauntered down the hall lost in thought, a patient called out to him for help. It turned out all he needed was some water and his call button wasn't working. Jack ended up visiting with him for forty-five minutes and then stopped by another half-dozen rooms throughout the morning. It seems everyone wanted someone to talk to, someone to listen. He immediately saw that it didn't take a lot of extra work to give patients what mattered most to them.

It's not like Jack had lost sight of the patients before that morning—he just started seeing things more clearly through their eyes. The new insights moved him enough to regularly schedule "administrative rounds."

Every patient he talked to had different things to say, but the conversations almost always led back to fear. He expected that, but he didn't expect the source of what really frightened them. Of course, those having critical surgeries or dealing with terrifying diseases had the innate fear that comes with the territory. But a lot of the folks he met were more afraid of people just not paying attention to them than anything else. They needed to believe in the people who were taking care of them. They wanted to know that everyone was working together on their behalf, and that the left hand knew what the right hand was doing.

It didn't take a rocket scientist, or even a brain surgeon, to realize that giving patients the peace of mind they needed so badly was the most important thing he could do, not to mention the obvious benefits of having a patient with a positive outlook.

Another thing that really surprised him was how much he enjoyed talking with the terminal patients. For the most part they wanted to talk to anyone who would listen. They wanted to tell their stories, to tell him what they knew, and listen to what he knew. Most of them craved interaction. After a few visits, they told him that their discussions together made it easier for them to talk to their families about their situations. They didn't teach him this in medical school. This was something that could only be learned by getting to the bedside and listening.

He wasn't sure where to start and how to do it, but he realized that any strategy he came up with to improve the hospital must not only include the patients, it had to start with giving them what they needed most. He realized a little down the road that basing everything he did on what mattered most to patients was probably the best diagnosis he'd ever come up with.

With the NEI just hours away, Jack walked the floors of the hospital hearing the same things he had heard in Billings, which gave him great comfort and confidence...almost enough to allay his fears. It's not that he expected anything different in Seattle, but taking on this job was considered a big move from where he came from, and he needed a little validation that no matter how many beds, or how large a staff, this hospital was no different than the smallest rural Montana hospitals he visited during his residency. They all had patients who needed the same thing. And changing a small country hospital or this urban behemoth began with one relationship at a time.

THIRTY-TWO

When Ben's brain switched to awake, he reached over to feel Mel next to him, only to find her gone. He thought it was Monday, the one day of the week they actually had the same shift hours, but maybe the hospital had called her in. Then he heard her start up the coffee grinder.

"Get out of bed, lazybones, your cappuccino's almost ready and we have a big day today."

Ugh. "Every day's a big day."

"We also have that NEI thing today."

"Great! Thanks for reminding me."

Mel sat down across from him at their little kitchen bistro table and gave him her "I mean business" expression.

"What?"

"Ben, I've been doing a lot of thinking on this and I need you to know that as much as I love you and want to be with you, I need to know that you're going to do the right thing in this meeting."

"Come on, Mel, I always try to do the right thing."

"Trying isn't enough this time. I told you how I feel about your allegiance to all things Lang and that you're really in denial about it."

"Do we have to have this conversation right now?"

"Ben, we can stop talking about it, but you have to know that I can't live with someone who doesn't respect what I do and doesn't respect himself."

"What the hell are you talking about? Of course I respect what you do."

"Do you? We'll see."

"And of course I respect myself...okay, mostly respect myself. Yes, I do kiss Lang's butt every day, but that's just a smart business strategy. Life's all about paying dues to get what you want. That's how this business works."

"Then you better really decide what you want, Ben. Because every step you take closer to Ethan Lang is a step away from me. Remember what I said, if we can't be on equal footing..."

With that she put her dish in the sink and headed for the shower.

THIRTY-THREE

NEVER EVENT INVESTIGATION II

Jane Carolli didn't know how this meeting was going to turn out. Jack had told her that Lang would show up for at least thirty minutes, and that pretty much guaranteed everything would remain business as usual. Normally, she'd be thinking how it really didn't matter how the vice president for Medical Affairs performed, but today, surprisingly, Jane was beginning to feel deeply invested in Dr. Jack Martin and his ideas. She needed him to succeed.

Dr. Ethan Lang entered the room irritated. Irritated at caving in to Martin and for not immediately recognizing his brown-nose effort to get him there. Although he had no surgeries until later in the afternoon, he would rather have his wisdom teeth put back in and ripped back out than sit through the meeting.

Jane, Julie, Mel, Ben, Dr. Zeller, the anesthesiologist, and Jack Martin rounded out the room. Jack had given Dr. Hartley a pass, believing he couldn't really add anything to the meeting and would only act as insulation and validation for Lang. If a group photo could have been snapped right before starting, the caption might have read, "Screw the coffee...five mgs of morphine all around."

Jack Martin began. "Okay, everyone, thanks for coming, let's get this thing started. First, I want to tell you what we want to accomplish. I would like to dissect what happened from a different perspective. Let's work together to determine what exactly happened so that we can avoid a repeat and determine if a checklist or safety sheet is really what we need. Let's look at this from a curative perspective so that we don't waste time creating a new kind of Band-Aid that merely treats a reoccurring symptom. Does anyone want to say anything before we get going?"

You could have heard a fly fart.

"Okay, I'm going to start with Dr. Zeller as he missed the last..."

"Wait a second," interrupted Dr. Lang. "You said I would be out of here in thirty minutes. I'm going first so that I can get out of here and maybe do something important the rest of the day."

No one was surprised.

"Okay, Dr. Lang. I'm starting out asking everybody the same thing. Just tell me what you saw that day, how you felt about it, and what you could have done differently."

"How I felt about it? Are you kidding? So then we can all get up arm-in-arm, sing Kumbaya and roast marshmallows? Okay, for the last time, this is what happened. A stupid pimply-faced transcriptionist screwed up. Some inexperienced nurses weren't forceful enough in bringing it to my attention, and I cut out the wrong lobe. This isn't about checklists and procedures; it's simply a matter of people not doing their jobs properly. I don't know whether it's a personal lack of commitment or poor training, but maybe if we cleaned house a little bit, we could come up with a more competent support staff. God knows that would make my job much easier. We're done."

"Before you go, Dr. Lang, I've got to get your opinion on one thing. I recognize the influence you carry around here, and I know of your brilliant surgical record. It just seems to me, with no disrespect, that you're blaming things on the inexperience of others, which is not what I intended this meeting to do. Shouldn't the patient, Edie, be the centerpiece of this conversation? It seems to me that regardless of what your surgical report said, and what credence you gave or did not give the nurses, shouldn't every surgeon take a few seconds to look at the scans before operating, if only to be the best possible advocate for our patients?"

"Garbage," snapped Lang. "When I'm surrounded by idiots, bad things will happen. And, Jane, you better rein in your boy and tell him how things work around here if he plans on lasting the month. I'm done."

"Hold on, Dr. Lang," said Carolli. "Ethan, I understand that you don't want to participate, but we lost a patient and this is important. You can have a pass and not participate, but I'd really appreciate it if you just stay and listen."

Lang was caught off guard. Was Carolli standing up to him? She didn't order him to stay, or he'd already be gone. She was probably trying to save face in front of her new hire. *Fine,* he thought, *he'd give her a little rope, but she was getting very close to reaching his limits of tolerance.*

"Fine, Jane. I'll sit here, but leave me out of it."

Jack Martin didn't miss a beat. "Okay, Dr. Zeller, same question. Tell me what you saw that day, how you felt about it, and what you could have done differently."

Zeller, a sixty-something, been-there-done-that kind of guy, seemed unfazed by the question or Lang's mini-tirade.

"From my end, this surgery was as ordinary as it gets. I performed my normal job routine, evaluation of possible drug conflicts, putting her under, monitoring vitals, fluid needs—you all know what I do."

"Go on."

"The one problem I vaguely remember was some nurse saying something and a short disagreement ensuing. I stay pretty focused on my patient, so I don't remember much more than double-checking the surgical orders with the ink written on the patient's torso. They both said the same thing, so I assumed the physician was correct and we moved on."

"How did that make you feel?"

"I have no idea what you are after when you say that. The physician prevailed because the physician is almost always right. Experience triumphs over inexperience."

"You don't remember what the nurse said?"

You could almost see the steam escaping from Lang's ears.

"What do you want from me, Dr. Martin? I was concentrating on my patient's vitals and told you all I remember. As far as what I would do differently, absolutely nothing. Now may I leave? I have a case in a couple of hours and need to get some sustenance."

Jane Carolli chimed in again, "Please bear with us for a short while longer. Thank you."

"I'd like to go next," said Julie, imperceptibly angling her back toward Lang.

Jack quickly surveyed the group. Ben Waller was fidgeting but hanging in there, and neither Mel nor Jane Carolli had any objections. Lang showed the emotion of a paperweight.

"Okay, Julie, thank you. Same question. What did you see that day, how did you feel about it, and what could you have done differently?"

Barely composing herself, Julie said, "I followed protocol to a T. Let me first say, not only do I always follow protocol with every patient, I was particularly invested in Edie. Yes, I know we shouldn't say things like that, but we got to know each other. She had an infectious personality. I'm not saying that I was more thorough with her than anyone else, but I was as thorough as anyone could have been."

"That's fine, Julie, no problem. Now what about the morning of the surgery?"

"Everything was going along normally when Dr. Lang came in and got down to business. Most surgeons I work with want to see the scan prior to cutting. So I naturally looked at it and then looked back at the markings on Edie's torso. The two didn't jibe, so I asked Dr. Lang if he would check out the scan. He said no, and told me to just do my...well he said no."

"This is garbage," shot Lang.

Jack Martin hesitated, and then said, "Dr. Lang, having a different perspective is just that. If you want to reply to what Julie says, please do. Everybody, please let's not lose sight of the fact that everyone's job affects everyone's job. Let's hear Julie out, and then the floor's yours if you want it, Dr. Lang."

Lang stared down at the table and Julie hesitated, and then continued.

"I tried my hardest to point out the problem again, but nobody listened. The way I was spoken to really shook me up, so I just shut up and prayed that I was wrong. As far as how I felt—scared to death, and in this case, literally scared for Edie's life...and my career."

Ben thought that he probably should have been quiet, but it came out of him before he even knew it; "Julie, if you really knew you were right, why didn't you do something more drastic? You could've stopped that surgery if you wanted to."

"Ben," muttered Mel.

Julie replied, "Dr. Waller, you weren't there. I knew I was right. You don't know what it's like to face up against a physician. In all honesty, you guys scare me and maybe I was too intimidated and that cost Edie her life. Maybe it was my fault."

"That's the first thing you got right," said Lang.

"Hold on," said Jack. "This isn't about blame or fault, and it wasn't yours or any one person's. Let's just try to figure it out so it doesn't happen again."

"Easy for you to say, Dr. Martin. When I found out I was right about the scans, I felt a combination of vindication and powerlessness. I've been having nightmares ever since." With that, Julie let the dam loose and buried her head in her hands.

"Let's take five minutes to get some coffee and then get back to it."

Lang was out of the room before everyone exhaled.

Mel immediately went to comfort Julie, but not before giving Ben a look that would have scared a moray eel back into its hole.

THIRTY-FOUR

Walking out of the meeting room, Ben was tempted to go back to his office and manufacture an emergency, allowing him to miss the rest of the meeting. He thought Lang was being obstinate, but he also understood where he was coming from. He wasn't sure this meeting was going to do anything for anyone. If they really wanted to change things, they should just have fewer meetings.

"Ben, what the hell were you thinking?"

"Mel, jeez, don't sneak up on me like that."

"Look, Ben, I know that's not you in there. Julie was barely holding it together, to the point of blaming herself for the entire incident. Do you know how brave it was for her to stand up to Lang? And you got on her case?"

"Whoa, Mel, I did no such thing. I just thought that if I were in her place, I would have shouted and thrown things, if I really believed in what I found. I really can't blame Lang for ignoring her."

"Really? Well, why do you think Lang ignored her, besides the fact that he's a first-class jerk?"

"She asked for it. Okay, fine. Lang is a physician. He has more education, experience, and the most to lose."

"I thought Edie had the most to lose. And even if the rest of that is true—even if he is the smartest guy in the room, does that negate everyone else's experience? Is he smarter and more experienced than everyone in the room combined just because he has an 'MD' after his name?"

"Obviously not, Mel, but I wasn't there, so all of this is conjecture and there's not much value in arguing over something we both didn't see."

"That's easy, isn't it, Ben? I'll tell you one thing I do know. As much as I care for you, I may have been wrong about you from the start. I thought I saw some things in you that just may not be there."

"Wait a second, like what?"

"Like the ability to put your ego aside, and when necessary get off your high horse and admit that some of us less fortunate non-physicians really know what we're doing. And while I'm at it, it's pretty disgusting to witness your ridiculous fear of Ethan Lang and how you let him dictate your professional life."

"That's not fair. I don't think of you people that way, and Lang's a colleague and integral to my practice."

"You people?"

"Great, Mel, I totally respect what you and other nurses do. It's just hard for you to understand because you didn't go to medical school."

"You better hope that perspective is worth losing me for, because I'm not sticking around if you don't revisit your priorities. You're as complicit as Lang in everything you do. You have him up on a pedestal and justify his actions because he's the number-one admitter in this place and puts money in your pocket. Please think, smart guy, how much good did Lang's rainmaker status do for Edie? Stimulus and response, Ben—all he had to do was take ten seconds to look at the damn scan before cutting. Ten seconds and Edie would be alive today. And this is the guy you're defending? We gotta get back."

And she left him standing there both angry and worried. He didn't want to lose her. She couldn't be serious. He knew they could work out this stuff. Ben didn't think he'd fallen this hard, but he didn't want to be without Mel in his life. Yet he couldn't do what she wanted him to, even if he agreed. She didn't get the fact that he had to kowtow to Lang or he wouldn't have a career here. Everything wasn't as black and white as she saw it.

THIRTY-FIVE

With just Ben, Melanie, Julie, and Jane Carolli left at the meeting, Dr. Jack Martin began right where he had left off.

"Okay, Melanie, I know you weren't in the OR, but Edie was your patient and I understand you've been mentoring Julie for a while...so how did you feel about it, and is there anything you could have done differently to change the outcome?"

"I don't think so. Julie and I happened to talk just minutes after the surgery ended, and another time the next morning after the incident was validated. She followed protocol. She went by the surgical chart and admitting diagnosis, and was the one who drew the marks on Edie's torso. She believed in the paperwork just like everyone else, until she looked at the scans."

For the first time in the meeting, Jane Carolli interrupted. "Yes, Ms. Swift, we know from a number of different sources that Julie was doing her job, but do you have anything new that will help us? Because right now, I've heard our lead surgeon say that Julie wasn't forceful enough about the scan, and our anesthesiologist remembered some conflict, but nothing exact. How do you explain that?"

Jack cut in, "Ms. Carolli, please remember that the object of this meeting is not to blame or punish, but to save lives in the future based on what went wrong here."

"I realize that, Dr. Martin, but these inconsistencies need further explanation, don't you think?"

Jack let her question hang in the air, which gave Jane a few seconds to think about the coaching road she was going down and she sat back in her chair saying nothing. She thought to herself, *Old habits die hard. Pausing before responding to stimulus isn't as easy as it sounds.*

Melanie didn't wait for Jack to answer, "Wait a second here. It seems to me that if we get into a he-said-she said argument, nobody wins."

"You're right," said Jack. "So what should we be discussing, Melanie?"

"I'm not sure, I just know that there is something else going on around here. I don't know you well, Dr. Martin, but since you've arrived, you keep bringing up the patient as the common denominator, and it seems that if we all thought about that a little more, and less about ourselves, Edie would still be here."

Hesitantly, Ben said, "Wait a second, Mel. You almost sound like we all don't put our patients first. Every physician in this hospital, including Dr. Lang, is here for the patients. All of us are."

Mel couldn't resist, "Listen to you defending Dr. Lang, Ben."

"Wait, wait, wait," Jack interrupted. "Mel, I like where you were headed, but again, let's try not to make any of this personal so that we can work together to find an answer."

"So, Mel," continued Jack, "do you have anything else to add, because I would also like to hear Dr. Waller's thoughts."

"Again, Dr. Martin, I have no idea what we should do or what we could have done differently other than following your idea of taking a minute to really consider the circumstances before responding. But I do know that people ignore each other inside that surgical suite every day, and in every corner of this hospital. And it's the patient who obviously loses."

Ben couldn't help but think that Mel was waiting for him to hang himself. He agreed that they had a ton of stuff going on. Everyone was pretty overwhelmed just doing their jobs and not getting into trouble, him included. His best bet was to not comment on what Mel said and just tell it as he saw it.

"I also was not in the room during the surgery, so all I can do is tell you what I remember. From the beginning, when I first got the news of Edie's diagnosis from Dr. Hartley, I'm pretty sure that he said she needed her right superior lobe removed, not the inferior. But again, this is all from memory."

"When I read the report just before surgery, I thought that I must have been mistaken, but I said nothing, because again, I had no real evidence other than my bad memory. But I didn't worry about it, knowing that they'd figure it out in surgery. There are plenty of safeguards and Lang would probably look at the scan. Maybe I should have compared the scan to the report prior to the surgery, but that's not my job. Maybe we do need a checklist or a couple of new initiatives."

"Anything else to add, Ben?"

"I'm done."

Jack agreed, "You're right, Ben, it may not be your job. But is doing our job the only thing we're responsible for around here? What about the way we listen to each other?"

"I don't follow."

"There are varying degrees of listening that range from simply hearing all the way to giving one's complete attention without judgment."

Again, a fly fart would have been deafening.

Ben then asked, "What do you mean by listening without judgment?"

"Look, Ben," said Jack, "we've all been in conversation and unintentionally began to think about the next thing we were going to say before the other person even finished talking. And sometimes, we rush to judgment about what we think they're going to say...leading us to make invalid assumptions. I'm saying that really hearing someone out, and listening more from a learning stance, eliminates rushing to judgment and making assumptions on unreliable information."

Jack Martin let it sink in for a few seconds before continuing. "And, Ben, think of what effect responsible listening plays in teamwork. Because what happened to Edie was a group—or I should say, a team–failure. We're here today because all of us had preconceived notions and didn't take the time to listen without judgment."

"Can't argue with that," said Ben. "But it still seems like it's our fault... meaning, as individuals we all failed."

Jane Carolli spoke next. "Dr. Waller, we can beat ourselves up as individuals, but what's the value in that? We've been trained in a ridiculously competitive environment, and the entire hospital continues to promulgate individualism because nobody knows anything different. No one person can possibly be thrown under the bus under these circumstances."

"Fair enough," said Ben.

Carolli continued, "Dr. Waller, you said that Dr. Lang could've worked better together with Julie, and was maybe negligent for not double-checking the scan regardless of whether or not the nurse said anything?"

Julie winced.

"I just said that in a perfect world I thought he could have caught it before he started, but it wasn't really his fault. I think Dr. Lang was a victim here. He could've checked the scans, but he's been operating off of information from Dr. Hartley's charts for years without a hitch. He believed in the surgical report, which he should have, and he was let down."

Mel barely contained herself. "Lang a victim. And what was Edie, chopped liver? I can't believe what I'm hearing."

Jack Martin calmly took over the room. "Let's re-evaluate for a minute. We obviously have some differences of opinion as to what happened and who is at fault; let's think about what we can all agree on for a minute."

"Do you all agree that regardless of why or who, people weren't working together in the operating room?"

There were muted "Yeses" with no disagreements.

"Do you all agree that this lack of ability to listen to each other is bigger than this incident and needs to be addressed?"

He kept going. "So yes, I think we should revisit a surgical checklist, but that will just cure this particular scan symptom. We need to deal with the underlying cause."

"And what would that be, Dr. Martin?" said an emboldened Julie.

"That we all need to realize that there is something bigger than just doing our job, and that all of us need to feel safe enough to express our opinions."

Ben couldn't help himself, "That seems a little unrealistic."

Mel countered, "Only if you want it to be, Ben."

"Exactly," said Jack Martin. "Not to pick on you, Dr. Waller, but nothing is attainable without community buy-in and acceptance. Acceptance that things are broken and acceptance that things can get much better."

Jack let that hang in the air for a minute before saying, "I would like to schedule one more meeting to move this forward. I think we need to talk about how we are all showing up around here focused only on our jobs, and how our jobs affect each other, especially the patient. We also need to start thinking in terms of our organizational roles as well. That's the first step in avoiding this problem in the future. In the meantime, I would like to ask Ms. Swift and Dr. Waller to meet with me concurrently to look at the existing pre-surgery checklist and see what we can do to amend it. Let's meet again next week, if you have no objections, Jane?"

"Not at all."

When nobody jumped in, the meeting ended itself and everyone instantly retired to their corners of the hospital.

THIRTY-SIX

Jane Carolli stopped Dr. Martin walking down the corridor and asked him for a follow-up for a minute in her office. She had surprised herself during the meeting by standing up to Dr. Lang and it felt good. She knew it was risky, but hey, no pain no gain. She definitely saw some tiny glint of light trying to break through the cracks Jack Martin had caused. But she had to move slowly and deliberately, knowing that Ethan Lang still had the power to make her life miserable.

"Well, Jane, what did you see in there?"

"Almost too much to comprehend. It totally amazes me that we all work in the same place and see things so differently."

"Yes, it's apparent that this place is comprised of a bunch of individuals doing their own thing. But what did you think about readjusting how we think about our jobs and how what we do here fits into the bigger organizational picture?"

"That was great, Jack, and I want to talk more about that, but what I really find interesting is that Ben Waller, a once-clear Lang disciple, seems a bit conflicted, probably due to the influence of Melanie Swift. And I think we can leverage that."

"Jane, I have to respectfully disagree. You're going down the wrong road. This isn't about assertive training, Ethan Lang, or any one individual. I realize he's a problem for you, but there's a much bigger problem and that's how unsafe everyone feels around here. People feel so threatened that they won't even follow through when they know they're right and someone's life hangs in the balance. We have to make it a safer place to communicate. And when it comes to Dr. Lang, maybe we can deal with him by not dealing with him at all."

"What do you mean?"

"If we can invest most everyone else in what we're talking about, then we can move forward whether Lang likes it or not. Jane, you'll be doing yourself a great service when you start admitting that you, your participation, and backing, is the key to making this thing work. Not Lang. This will only work if it trickles down from the top, and you are the top, whether you feel it or not."

"I know, Jack. Bring it on."

"Great, because you have the perspective that he doesn't. If I asked Lang what needed fixing around here, he'd have a short list of problems that have plagued us forever. Maybe he'd bring up a pain-in-the-ass colleague or nurse, maybe he'd complain about a specific initiative. He doesn't see the big picture. He doesn't realize that the individual challenges he sees are symptoms of a culture-wide lack of communication and teamwork."

"But, Jack, we can't totally forget about how much influence he carries around here."

"Yes, he creates fear and uses it to influence everyone. But he's mostly interested in protecting physicians, and he only has power over anyone because they give it to him. Maybe we can start to initiate some changes around here regardless of his buy-in."

"How?"

"First, we can move forward without his blessing by not asking him to participate more than once."

"Go on."

"We can start to try to change things around here, ask him for his participation, and if or when he turns us down, we continue moving forward without him."

"He knows everything that goes on here, Jack. Almost every physician on staff is beholden to him one way or another."

"I know. It was the same way in Billings. A stubborn physician fought our changes the entire way until a lot of his colleagues saw potential in what we were doing and slowly joined us. He never did and fought us for months until he eventually gave up and moved on."

"I don't think Ethan Lang is ever going to roll over and move on from here. He's too close to retirement anyway."

"Maybe not, but again, we can base everything on what Lang will do, or on what we do. We can start showing everyone that there's a better way to show up to work every day. A better way to ensure we're giving patients what they need the most. And if Lang doesn't want to come along for the ride, it's his choice."

"All right, I'll operate from that perspective from here on out. What's our next step?"

"When we last spoke, we discussed what really bothers us most around here and what we'd like to see this place eventually become."

"Right, and how it all begins at the top, with me."

"Remember, Jane, how you act or don't act will determine what everyone else does. And after you, we're going to have to get some physicians invested in our cause. Regardless of your title, Jane, physicians are perceived as captains of the ship, and if we don't affect how they show up, we're dead in the water. So let's work on that agreement."

"Refresh my memory."

"You tell me, Jane, how you promise to show up, and I'll do the same for you."

"I'll start," continued Jack. "Remember, we talked about the criteria used to appraise or evaluate physicians? Up until now we judged them on their skills, getting things done, and their work ethic."

"Yes, but that's obviously not enough. We talked about needing to have team players that are approachable, which has nothing to do with how we currently evaluate staff."

"Right, approachable, along with being respectful and listening," added Jack.

"Listening without judging. Jack, what you and I want from our medical staff is the same thing our patients want from us."

"Right on, Jane. Absolutely. Just think how much more confident they would feel if they knew everyone who was taking care of them showed respect and really listened to each other?"

Jane let the thought hang in the air.

"Well, my first promise to you, Jane, is to try to be all of those things, all of the time."

"Although it shouldn't be, that sounds like a tall order, Jack."

"Wait, there's more," said Jane. "I think it's important for me to be reachable and respond quickly when you need something from me. And, I need to continue to concentrate on thinking before reacting. That sounds good—I'm up to creating some kind of a pact with you, it's just that I have no idea where to start."

"Look, Jane, you're already exhibiting new behaviors, including your willingness to learn and evolve."

"True. Okay, Jack, I promise to continue to stay in learning mode, which also means taking the time to think before I react."

"So in essence, you're willing to change your behavior?" asked Jack.

"Although I never realized my behavior was wrong, maybe I just didn't have the right attitude. Either way, yes, I'm promising to work on changing my behavior. I'd also love to be able to promise you something related to the teamwork aspect. I could sure use some teams working with me around here. Jack, how do we get people to start thinking about working together?"

"It's a process, Jane. Remember when we talked about the difference between our jobs and our roles, or how our jobs affect each other's?"

"Yes, right," Jane added. "Then I'm going to have to start teaching that concept to my senior execs and the MEC."

"One at a time, Jane. Just pick one executive to work with at a time."

Jane sat staring into space until Jack thought he could actually see the light bulb go on.

"I just don't know where to start, Jack. I'm going to have to model it by the way I lead, and by setting higher expectations that emphasize our roles, instead of just our jobs."

"Absolutely. And it won't take long for you to take on the coaching role that I'm playing with you. You're already capable of getting someone else to where we are now. I might just add that you'll continue to be available when I need you."

"Done."

"So let's review while I take some notes and write this thing up. I'm going to be your confidant, there for you as a sounding board."

"Go on."

"Like you, I'll be a role model, modeling the behaviors necessary to promote teamwork. And whenever we're talking, in person, or on the phone, you'll have my complete, undivided attention. Lastly, I'll trust and respect you now and in the long term. Sound good?"

"Yes. For my part," Jane looked down at her notes, "I'll continue to be open to learning. And I'll remember to put the patients first in my thoughts when designing all future leadership strategies. And of course, I'll do my best to trust and respect you. It's funny, Jack, I know this all makes sense, it just sounds so 'New Age' when I say it out loud."

"I know," he agreed, "maybe that's because as a CEO, you've been trained to focus on how you can improve the organization in terms of operational deficiencies, opposed to what we lack in relational skills. You've never been told that you're responsible for, or even capable of, assessing and actually designing working relationships. When I talk about coaching, that's a huge part of it...and one of the requisite skills needed to improve patient care."

"I get it, Jack. It makes sense...I just can't believe this is so new to me. What's next?"

"Like I said, it will start with us, then you'll pick our next candidate, and then we'll bring in the NEI group, since we already have a captive audience. We'll design a plan to slowly but surely bring the rest of the medical staff up to speed. Remember, it's not an overnight remedy. It's deliberate, but curative."

"Okay, thanks, Jack."

When Jack left the room, Jane seemed to breathe a little easier. She was sure this wasn't going to be easy, and not sure it would even work in the long run. The only thing standing in her way, besides her old self, was finding the time to do anything new. Most of every day was already spent managing people and conflicts. The next time they talked, she'd see what Jack had to say about having to manage things versus really showing the way as a leader. There just didn't seem to ever be enough time to do anything but put out fires.

THIRTY-SEVEN

Mel beat Ben home by an hour or so and immediately poured herself a glass of wine and settled into a hot bath. She had never felt so conflicted. Here was this great guy who treated her like a queen half the time, but his priorities seemed so out of whack.

Most of all, it bugged her that he was so afraid of Lang. Why couldn't he realize that his patients thought the world of him, and probably half of them came from patient referrals?

She didn't easily give in to emotions, but she started tearing up at the thought of moving out. Her threat to Ben was serious and it scared her. But she knew for sure that she couldn't stay with him if he didn't communicate with her as an equal.

The sound of the door interrupted her thoughts when Ben poked his head into the bathroom.

With a thin blanket of bubbles barely concealing her, he wanted to say whatever she needed to hear so he could jump into the tub. But he couldn't. It was in that split second he realized that he didn't know what to say or what he wanted. He knew he didn't want to lose Mel, but his fear of the uncertain future was overwhelming.

Lamely, he said, "How are you doing?"

"How do you think?"

"How about I slip in the tub with you and we put all this stuff behind us for the evening and just relax? We can talk about it tomorrow."

"Sorry. Not going to happen. You know I want you to be in this tub, Ben, but I wasn't kidding about how much this is hurting me. I can't do this if you don't make some changes."

"But, Mel, I'm not making up this stuff about Lang and my career."

"Ben, how many of your patients are referrals from other patients?"

"I don't know, maybe 30 percent. Why?"

"Because you can do this without Lang. It may be a slower road to where you want to go, but you can do it."

"Mel, Lang not only told his referral network to include me; he can bring me down by negatively campaigning against me. With a word, he could blacklist me with almost every physician on the staff and really impact my practice."

"Well then, why don't you work for the hospital and you wouldn't have to worry about it?"

"What made you say that?"

"I don't know. I just thought of it. It might be a way for you to get past your ties to Lang."

"Funny enough, I've been thinking about the same thing for a while."

"And you didn't want my opinion?"

"I just didn't want to tell anyone. I can't afford for Lang to find out, just in case I decide not to."

"And you think I would tell him?"

"Mel, it's not that I don't trust you, it's just how I've always been, how I've always needed to be to survive."

"Wow, Ben, you sound really paranoid and it doesn't flatter you. I think for right now, I could use a time-out."

"Really? Look, Mel, I think you're overreacting, but if that's what you need, I'll let you have it. I'll go to a hotel for a couple of nights and give you some space. Does that work for you?"

"Thanks, Ben, yes, I think that's a good idea."

Trying to be cute he added, "You'll be begging me to come home in a couple of days."

"Not until you work out a few things on your own. You not only need to decide whether you want to be aligned with the likes of Lang, but you should start thinking about how you really see me. Am I just a nurse, or an equal? If I don't have your complete respect, and feel like I'm at least an equal, equally as important to you as your work and the other physicians, then I don't know how we're going to make it."

"Fine."

THIRTY-EIGHT

Ben checked into the "W" downtown, thinking that a little luxury would feel good. It didn't.

The bed felt way too wide and sleep came in fits, but since medical school, he'd learned to go with very little.

Thoughts kept swirling through his head. *Am I really that afraid of Ethan Lang? I must look like such a wimp to Mel. Probably because I am one. I've always believed that life is about paying dues. Everything good must be paid for in advance and it's kind of a karma thing to me. I figure that taking the stuff I do from Lang is the only way I'll get the status I deserve at Angels.*

Could he make it without Lang? Mel was right about one thing—his patients seemed pretty pleased and they were referring. He knew he wanted Mel, but he had no idea what to do. As far as treating her as an equal, he actually did in most ways; it was just this physician thing. Since growing up under his father's wing, he'd seen physicians portrayed on a little higher level than everyone else. He didn't know how to overcome that, but since walking into the hotel room, he knew he had to figure it out. He really trusted her, and when he thought about it, as an adult, he didn't think he'd ever trusted anyone else.

His head was swirling. He trusted her; he just couldn't see her as an equal because of her lack of training. He had no idea what he should do. The only thing he knew for sure was that he didn't want to lose her and she was pretty right on about everything she was saying concerning Lang and the hospital... things were pretty screwed up.

He finally passed into a fitful sleep hoping that it was all a bad dream until the alarm sounded after what felt like ten seconds of sleep.

When he arrived at the office, Jack Martin was waiting outside his door, and for some reason unbeknownst to him, he wasn't all that irritated to see him there.

"Morning, Ben."

"Jack."

"I was hoping you'd give me a little feedback about what I said toward the end of the meeting, and I thought we could talk a little about where I'm hoping the next meeting will go."

"Only if we can do it on the way to the espresso stand. That hotel coffee didn't cut it for me."

He didn't intend for that to slip out.

"You stayed in a hotel last night?"

He guessed he could make up something, but for some reason, he continued.

"Mel and I had an argument about what's going on around here and how I treat her, and she felt we should retire to separate corners for a little while so I can supposedly figure out what I want."

"Do you know what you want?"

"Yes. Everything. I want Mel and I want to continue to build my practice."

"Sounds reasonable."

"Except that Mel can't stand how I kowtow to Lang, or more specifically, how she thinks I kiss his ass."

"That seems to be a pretty common malady around here."

"Well, there is a pecking order, and he thinks he's the top rooster."

"Only because we let him."

"Easy for you to say, Jack—he opened a lot of doors for me."

"Let me ask you this, what if people banded together and decided not to let his fear influence them?"

"A mutiny, how quaint. I can't imagine that happening."

"Let me rephrase. What if they all found something they believed in, something to rally around that made more sense to them than what they're doing now?"

"What are you talking about?"

"I'm talking about changing a few things around here so that the staff is more focused on giving patients what they need instead of purely surviving in this screwed-up system. There are a lot of good people here with their talents being wasted because they're working solo and just plain scared all the time. Imagine if everyone set most of their egos aside, combined their intelligence, and worked together to solve problems."

"Sounds like a nice dream. You'll need something more tangible to turn people against Lang."

"I don't think we need to think in terms of turning anyone against anyone, Ben. We just need to redirect focus, shift some perspectives. And if Lang doesn't want to join the effort, he'll be left behind."

"Again, I'm not sure how or what you're thinking of doing to make this little pipe dream of yours come true. I just can't see it happening here."

"Fair enough. Here's what I propose. I have a third NEI meeting scheduled for next week, and I'd like to use it to introduce this idea in tangible terms."

"I don't know Jack, that's not what an NEI is for."

"It isn't? I thought we clearly determined that Edie's death was caused from a staff so paralyzed by fear and set in their individual ways that they didn't do their jobs right. If Hartley had paused before answering and gave his transcriptionist five seconds of his time, the report wouldn't have been incorrect. If Lang had given Julie five seconds to look at the scan...Ben, do you remember the last thing I was talking about in the meeting yesterday?"

"That thing about how our jobs affect each other?"

"I'm impressed. Yes. If everyone connected to Edie's death thought about how what they did affected everyone else's jobs, we wouldn't be sitting here today either."

"That doesn't sound like the real world to me—more like a fantasy."

"I'd like to talk about how we can make it real. And all you need is an open mind. Jane Carolli's in. Anyway, whether you say it or not, all of you think these meetings are a waste of time, so why not humor me since you have to attend anyway?"

"Fine. It all sounds interesting, if far-fetched, but I still don't know if this has anything to do with my relationship with Lang. As much as I don't love the current set-up, I need his network to give me referrals, and not taking them won't change anything around here."

"Wouldn't it be nice if you could stop sucking on his teats."

"I beg your pardon."

"You know that the problems you're having around here are the same ones that sent you to a hotel?"

"What do you mean?"

"Why did she ask you to give her some space?"

"Partially because of my attitude about what's going on around here. She doesn't understand what it's like to be a physician."

"Go on."

"And also because she thinks I don't thoroughly trust her, that I don't treat her as an equal."

"Do you?"

"Not like she'd like me to, but I trust her as much as I've trusted anyone. Doesn't that count for anything?"

Jack put it back on him, "You tell me."

"Look, all of this relationship stuff isn't my strong suit. I was trained as a clinician, and that's my comfort zone."

"Me too, Ben. But the two aren't mutually exclusive."

"Are you saying I can learn to trust her, to treat her equally?"

"You can learn anything. All you have to do is apply what you learn daily."

"Sounds much easier said than done."

"Most things are. But that's what I want to begin talking about in the next meeting."

"I'm feeling kind of ambivalent here, Jack. I just want to get Mel back and have things run smoothly."

"You're capable of making both happen?"

"Probably, I just don't know how."

"Think for a second, Ben. Think about what's been going on around here and where you're staying tonight and tell me: is my approach worth a look-see if it will help you realize both of your goals?"

THIRTY-NINE

J ack left Ben staring into space like a deer in the headlights, starting to feel like he just might be opening up. Getting Mel fully invested seemed feasible, and if Mel got onboard, Julie would follow. Jane Carolli was Jack's biggest asset. She was really getting into it. She was even connecting the dots on her own. He just needed to offer continual coaching reinforcement.

After trying to get in touch with Mel all day, he finally ran into her in the cafeteria later that afternoon.

Mel sat lost in thought. She felt bad about kicking Ben out, but had needed to. Having worked as a nurse most of her adult life, she was resigned and disgusted about being treated like a second-class citizen. It made her feel like she wasn't trusted. Hospitals were a physician's world. She was just support staff. She got that. Thankfully, the patients never treated her that way. She put up with as much as she could at work, but she had to draw the line at home. She knew Ben was no different than most physicians. He had an ego. And he needed one to do what he did. Hell, we all do. But if she couldn't feel valued by him on both a professional and personal level, then this relationship was doomed.

"Ms. Swift, mind if I join you?"

She looked up, relieved that her thoughts had been interrupted. "Sure, Dr. Martin."

"Please, call me Jack. I need your help with the next NEI meeting."

"What can I say that I haven't already said?"

"We're not going to talk about the specifics of the event."

"Then why are we having a meeting? I thought we were going to write out a checklist."

Jack had never seen Mel looking so vulnerable. It was apparent her mind was elsewhere, probably on Ben, so he pressed on.

"We could, but I think there are more important things that need to be worked out first. Tell me something, aside from Ben, what drives you the craziest around here?"

She winced a little at the mention of Ben. "That could be a pretty extensive list. Probably the 'every-man-for-himself' attitude or just the way people treat each other with little respect half the time. But what does that have to do with Edie's NEI?"

"What if I was to tell you that what drives you crazy is a big part of why Edie died? And that although a new pre-op checklist is probably not a bad idea, it's still a partial solution that won't guarantee this won't happen again. It will only solve half the problem."

"What do you mean?"

"Shouldn't we be 100 percent sure of what we're doing to a patient well before they're anesthetized with a surgeon standing over them scalpel in hand?"

"Of course. But that's not possible with the kind of people we have around here. It's every man for himself."

"What about you, Mel? Are you that way too?"

"I have to be, Jack. I'm working alone here. Half the nurses on the floor don't talk to each other. I mean, they all join in on water cooler talk, you know, their personal stuff. But when it comes to work, it's pretty much 'Get out of my way and let me do my job.'"

"Where does the patient come into that equation?"

"Wait a second, I admit this place is pretty screwed up, but we're all here for the patients."

"I know that. But being here for the patients and basing everything on what the patients need are two different things. What if everyone communicated about what they were doing and worked more closely together? How would that affect patient care?"

"You know the answer to that, Jack. But that's never going to happen here."

"Why not?"

"Because nobody knows how to work together. They don't trust each other. Or maybe they don't believe that it's possible to let go of their egos and really work as a team?"

"That goes for you too?"

"Yes and no. It's not so black and white, is it? I mean, we have some pretty good people here, but there are also some arrogant, sanctimonious jerks, so it's difficult to figure out who's safe to talk to without risking a verbal beat down."

"Where does Ben fit into this?"

"I don't know. Talk about gray areas. I know he cares a lot about me. He listens to me, but he also seems to take a lot of what I say on the work front with a grain of salt. I want to trust Ben with my heart, but how can I when he doesn't show me the respect I deserve?"

She paused for a second and continued, "Pardon me for getting personal. I guess one thing shouldn't necessarily have to do with the other, but I'm pretty conflicted about a lot of things right now."

"Listen, Mel, I don't want to intrude into your personal stuff, but things like trust and respect are black and white, whether here, at home, or anywhere. I think that lack of respect you're feeling is the primary reason why Edie's case went the way it did. The staff involved in Edie's case didn't truly work as a team on her behalf. And I believe we have the opportunity and duty to do something about it before it happens again."

"How do we do that?"

"Regardless of how unreal a hospital full of people working together sounds to you, I believe it's possible from what I experienced in Billings. Things don't happen overnight, but they can change for the better."

"You think you're going to get people like Lang to trust each other...to work as team members? Please! Give me a break."

"Maybe not everyone is capable of changing. Maybe Lang will have to be left behind as the rest of us move forward."

"I would like to see that happen in my lifetime."

"Look, Melanie, I told you that I needed your help, and that begins with you having a little faith and humoring me for a while. I know that there's a tangible way of making things better around here and I'd like to get it in front of you guys. If this is going to work, I need you to listen to what I have to say."

"What can I do?"

"First off, you can go into the next meeting with an open mind."

"I can do that."

"Second, you can try to convince Julie and Ben to do the same."

"Julie's pretty screwed up right now, Jack. She'd love the idea, but, like me, I'm sure she'll be pretty skeptical."

"But, Melanie, if Julie had had a patient-centered team with her in the OR that day, Edie would have survived. Just the aspirational nature and putting it into context should connect with her."

"Of course it will, and I'll try my best to get her thinking positively about this. As for Ben, I'm sorry, Jack, but we're trying to work some things out and I don't think I can have much influence on his professional stance right now."

"I get that, Mel, and again, I don't want to intrude, but you already hinted that your personal problems are directly related to work and what I'm talking about may help with both. I need your help."

"I'll try. I just don't know what to do."

"Don't forget that just because we don't have the kind of culture we're talking about here, it doesn't mean we can't eventually design it. I know it sounds like a long, difficult process. And it is, but it moves exponentially faster with time. We're starting with small one-to-one relationships and building it out from there. Jane Carolli and I have already jumped in and are moving forward. Now you're getting involved. Eventually, we'll have enough people onboard to work as a small team. And then we'll recruit more small teams. Yes, it's a process. But we can do it."

FORTY

Jack Martin met Jane Carolli for drinks at the Hunt Club on Capitol Hill, where they could get a table in back and be left alone. He arrived first, then ordered a Manhattan when Jane arrived.

After the drinks came, Jane seemed intent on skipping the pleasantries, wanting to jump right in.

"Well, Jack, have you written everything up?"

He handed her the agreement. "Yep. Here you go."

Jane looked at it with admiration and bewilderment. It all made sense and she totally realized the need for it, but still saw the entire concept as somewhat of a long shot. Then she remembered that negative thinking accomplishes nothing. Although she was glad to move forward with this document–this pact–she still couldn't believe that the world, her world, turned out to be a place where you had to sign what practically amounted to a contract just to get along and work with each other. But she knew this was the right direction to go. If this worked, she could finally make some real positive changes around here. She signed the paper (Jack's signature was already affixed), and handed it back to him.

Jack said, "I'll make a copy and get it to you."

"Now what do we do, Jack?"

"We should talk a little more about how we got here and then how we're going to get the others—more specifically, a coalition of physicians—onboard."

"Keep going."

"When we first started talking, you kept bringing up your laundry list of problems. How all you do is put out fires, add more initiatives, and come up with Band-Aids that will keep our heads above water."

"That's my job."

"I know, and it's not your fault. Leaders everywhere face the same challenges. And if asked, they all know how far just treating the symptoms got them."

Jane paused before answering, "They have what I have. A staff that's disrespectful to each other...a bunch of individuals with bad attitudes who couldn't even fathom working together as a team. A lot of my people have just plain shut down."

"What happens when they shut down, Jane?"

"When people shut down it's discouraging and causes more bad attitudes, and so on. It's highly contagious."

"Okay, so we have this negative, self-perpetuating cycle. What caused it?"

"I don't know. It's always been this way everywhere I've worked. You tell me, Jack."

"Well, what's everybody focused on around here?"

"Their jobs and not getting into any trouble."

"What's wrong with that, Jane?"

Jane smiled. She realized what he was getting at and smiled at the simplicity of the answer.

"They're not looking at the bigger picture. How their jobs affect each other. It's much bigger than your job. If you only concentrate on doing your job, you might as well close your eyes, put in earplugs, and work in a vacuum."

Jack smiled, seeing Jane turning the corner.

"Okay, I get it. This cycle we've fallen into comes from not realizing how our jobs, or the parts we play around here, affect each other, and how beneficial it would be if we all knew what our colleagues were doing, and why."

Jane continued, "You and I managed to break the cycle, so how do we get everyone else to do it? You see, Jack, I am so overwhelmed that I would paint myself pink and run around naked if I thought it would help my efforts around here. We're just two people, and you're the only one in this hospital who has actually seen this concept work."

Jack paused. "Sorry, Jane, I'm just trying to get past the pink and naked comment. I'll get to you being overwhelmed in a minute—let's just finish this thread. You're right, there's just the two of us. But you're the boss, and just about every big change that happens anywhere begins with an idea and a grassroots movement to help it along."

"Agreed. But like you said, we need to get the physicians onboard or we're sunk. How did you get them interested in what happened in Montana?"

"Jane, once I had the leadership onboard, we began to help all the physicians understand their roles as coaches. Every good team needs a coach, and all of our patients expect us to work in teams on their behalf. They don't want to wonder whether we're all on the same page, they want to experience it through every interaction they have. Yes, we physicians need to show up as proactive leaders as well, but that's secondary if you really want to improve patient care."

Jane replied, "I get what you're talking about with the coaching, Jack, that's what you're doing with me right now."

"Right, obviously, since you're the boss, I'm not telling you to do things, I'm coaching you. I learned in Billings that good leaders not only coach their teams and staff, they slowly but surely train them to coach as well. They learn to ask the right questions so people can come to realizations themselves. Do you think that could happen here?"

Jane looked a little pleased, saying, "With the patient as the true motivation behind everything, sure, that sounds doable. It only makes sense. What else?"

"We need to give them a blueprint to move forward based on something they're already comfortable with. Bear with me, Jane. Why did you get onboard for our little agreement?"

"Because the process gave me a picture of where we are and where we should be going. It gave me some hope."

"Try to break it down for me, pretend that I'm from Mars or something."

"You kind of are, Jack," she smiled. "Well, we clearly defined where we are today and how we got here. And the easy part, we figured out where we want to go. But what do we have to do to get us there? What's the reason we're stuck in this negative cycle?"

"C'mon, Jane, you tell me."

"We have to get everyone to think past just doing their jobs, and start looking at the roles they play here at Angels. I know this sounds kind of funny, but along with job descriptions, maybe we should be talking about role descriptions. I mean, we all may have different jobs, but for this hospital to really change for the better, we all have to play the same role."

"You're on the right track, Jane. And this role has to be based on how we behave with each other."

Jack continued, "To figure out where we are, where we're going, why we are where we are, and how we get to where we want to be..."

Jane broke in, "That's a mouthful."

He smiled. "This is what we came up with in Billings. We just fit what you just so eloquently expressed into a framework physicians rely on every day. To define where we are today and where we want to go is akin to doing a history and physical—follow me?"

"Keep going."

"Discovering the 'why' or the root cause of our problems is like giving a differential diagnosis. Then, educating them so they know their organizational roles, their role description as coaches, is the treatment. And everything we did led to giving the patients what they needed the most: to trust that we're all working together on the same page."

"That makes sense. It reminds me of the nursing assessments we used to do."

"Jane, in all candor, you took to this pretty quickly. We can't try to force all of this down Waller, Hartley, and Zeller's throats, even if it has a familiar feel to it."

"And especially Lang."

"Yeah, I don't know how he'll react. I'm willing to bet he'll see the merits, but I don't know that at this point in his career he'll have any interest in changing a thing. But we can't focus on that. The only chance we have, Jane, is to be very deliberate. Can you do that?"

"I want to, Jack, and I know I can, but as I mentioned earlier, I spend most of my days managing people, problems, and putting out fires. How do I add this to the mix and still get everything else done?"

"Maybe you need to look at your own role as a leader a little more closely."

"What do you mean, Jack?"

"Well, let's define leadership for a minute."

"That's easy, I'm in charge. Which really means that I'm responsible for fixing and maintaining everything that goes on around here."

"Jane, that sounds like managing—only being responsible for controlling or administering."

Jane interrupted. "You bet I'm responsible for controlling and administering everything around here. I am a manager. If I don't manage, who will?"

"Seems like I hit a nerve. No need to be defensive. Yes, you do need to manage things to some extent. But to lead comes with the responsibility of showing your organization the way. Which brings me back to coaching."

"Again, that sounds wonderful, and it's just how I would like to see myself, but I have to be a manager."

"Yes, you do, but they're not mutually exclusive. Maybe, if we continued to spread what the two of us have accomplished throughout the ranks and help get everyone to show up with some leadership coaching behaviors, some of your management problems wouldn't make it up the ladder to you, and you'd have more time to lead and institute some of your own ideas."

Jane paused a few seconds. "It's so obvious in a way, but this is all I've ever known, all we were taught. And not only that, being CEO here has taken me too far from the bedside. I've integrated the patients into my leadership quotient, but I haven't based the foundation of my decision-making process on what matters most to them. I know I'm a good administrator—it's just human to question things sometimes."

"Jane, you're still the same good person with good ideas that you've always been. When you play the CEO part, you haven't lost any of your nursing skills and instincts. You're still the eager college coed, the nursing student. Everything we were, we still are. It's all still in us. It's about summing up your past experiences and outlooks and combining them with some new sensibilities that allow you to be who you want to be, instead of leaving it to others to define you. Forget about what the norm has dictated up to this point."

"I love the thought of that, Jack, but I'll feel better when it's more than just the two of us walking down this path."

"We'll get them, Jane. One or two at a time, but we'll get them."

FORTY-ONE

When Dr. Ethan Lang's secretary announced an unscheduled visit from Jack Martin, he let out a resigned sigh and thought that he really needed to get out on his boat. He wasn't sure what Martin and Jane Carolli had in mind, and he had less than zero interest in finding out. He had already made up his mind that he would retire in two years and there was no value for him in changing the status quo in any way, shape or form.

"Sure," he said. "Let him in."

"Dr. Lang, thanks so much for giving me a few minutes. I'm sure your schedule is pretty tight, so I'll be quick."

"You have two minutes."

"Have you given any thought to our discussion about physicians' roles as leaders around here?"

"Martin, I really don't have time for this. I don't need to think about being a leader. I am, and everyone knows it. I don't see much point discussing it any further."

Jack hated to stoop to the leverage game, but desperate times call for... "Physician to physician, give me just a few minutes to ask you a couple of questions. The sooner you let me, the sooner I'll be gone."

Lang was thinking that Martin was headed for "really gone," and didn't even know it. "Fine, ask."

"What do you think is the most important thing to the physicians at Angels?"

"Obviously, doing good work and making people well again."

"So doing a good job is enough?"

"I don't follow you."

"What about the parts we play in the entire organization?"

"Look, we do our jobs and save lives."

"True, but when I say 'parts,' I'm referring more to how doing our jobs affects other people doing their jobs. Independent of our jobs, we do have an organizational role in common. Don't you agree?"

"I don't really know what you're talking about. And since you're running out of time, I don't think I really care to."

"Dr. Lang, regardless of the fact that you're captain of the ship in the OR, we all have jobs to do. The thing is, we're all so focused on doing them well that it impacts our ability to work as a team."

Ethan Lang couldn't argue with the premise, but he wasn't going to let this thing go down as physician error.

"Martin, team or no team, this may have been a communication error, but it wasn't caused by one of the physicians involved. Do I have to make that clear every time I talk to you?"

"No," said Jack, confronting Lang for the first time, "because, as I've said a number of times, I'm not looking to blame anyone. I'm just trying to clearly define the root cause of the problem and ensure it doesn't happen again."

"Wow, showing a little backbone are we? Okay, I get it. Do what you think you have to do in the meeting, but don't expect me to raise my hand like a schoolchild and participate. You're wasting my time now and you'll be wasting it then. We're done here."

Lang looked down at his desk and told Jack to get lost without having to say a word.

Jack headed for the door, thinking that he had lost control there for a second. But maybe in this case, it was a good thing.

FORTY-TWO

Having avoided Mel all day, Ben hoped he could go back home that night. But he found a note on his locker that read, "Ben, I still haven't changed my mind and need you to not come back to the house tonight. I need a little more time, unless you've re-thought things. Mel."

How long is this going to last? He texted her and asked her to meet him for a drink so they could at least talk about it, and she asked him to meet her for a "quick bite" and a glass of wine at Place Pigalle overlooking the waterfront.

He got there a little early and ordered a nice Bordeaux, a couple of salads, and a cheese board. Mel walked through the door just after they had brought everything to the table.

He started to get up and she came over and kissed him briefly before he could stand up, "Don't get up, Ben. Wow this looks great, you read my mind."

"I've missed you, Mel."

"I've missed you too, but I feel strongly that things have to change, Ben. This isn't a whim. I've really thought about this."

"I understand, Mel, I just want to talk and try to figure some things out."

"How about we start with what really bothers me—not that you're afraid of Lang, or that you think you need him, but how you can't seem to give me the respect I need from you."

He couldn't stand it when she called him out on being afraid.

"Mel, I told you that I respect you more than anyone I've ever met. Doesn't that count for anything?"

"Of course. Maybe instead of trying to determine how much respect is enough, we should be looking for the underlying issue?"

"What do you mean?"

"Whether at work or not, you've obviously had issues for a long time.

Maybe we can discover the source and figure this thing out."

"How do you suggest we do that, Dr. Freud?"

"Jack Martin and I were talking about how much we need mutual respect at work. How important it is to know everyone else's roles, so we can best do our jobs."

"Jack, Jack, Jack! I like this guy, Mel, and he makes sense. But although this isn't rocket science, it isn't exactly easy, Mel."

"Nobody said anything about easy, Ben."

"Okay, then let's talk about work for a second. I do my job the best I can, and without wanting to sound like a jerk, I do it well."

"There you go, getting all defensive. Yes, you do a good job, but not the best you could be doing. None of us do, as long as we work in a vacuum."

"What do you mean?"

"I mean that we have all this combined experience and brainpower that we never use around here. And along with the frustration that comes with people not being heard, not being able to contribute the way they want to, we can't possibly be doing what's best for patients."

"That's just how it is in this business, Mel. It's never really been a team sport. I mean, sure, we call each other in for consults, assist each other, and cover for each other, but since my first days of medical school, being a physician has always meant depending on yourself, and more importantly, protecting yourself."

"Listen to yourself. Is walking around paranoid, blind to the periphery, best for your patients?"

Okay, he thought, *she kind of has me there. But she's not living in the real world if she thinks I can change what's been going on forever.*

"Mel, I didn't create this system—why do you think I can change things?"

"Ben, I'm not asking you to change the system. I am just saying that we can change as individuals. Change has to start one person at a time. I just want to work in a place where I'm doing the best I can for my patients. And that means listening to others and others listening to me. It means combining our know-how instead of being so adversarial. Don't you think that would make a difference?"

"Of course it would, it just seems a little out of the reality realm, given what it's like and always has been like around here. I am not really against anything you say—I just don't know what I can do to make you change your mind and let me come home."

"Ben, you just said that you are not against what I am saying. I need you to be more committed to it, to be on the same page, to believe that change is not only possible, but necessary. I need you to stop letting the past dictate how you are today. Jeez, Ben, we're young, can't we change? Are we no longer capable of seeing and doing things differently?"

"I don't know what to say to that, Mel. I can't find anything wrong with what you're saying—I just can't figure out what I can personally do to change things. I am having a real hard time seeing the upside for me. Going against Lang could be career suicide."

"Listen to yourself...me, me, me. We both got into this for the same reasons, for the people, our patients. And all you can talk about is your career. I need you to see past your job, Ben. I need you to see the bigger picture."

"I get where you're coming from, Mel. It's time for me to move back in, and you can help me figure this out."

"Look, Ben, you have this idea that physicians live on a completely different level than everyone else. And in some ways, you're right. You do have more training and have gone through hell to get here...but we're all equal when it comes to the patients. I get it, Ben. I get how you were trained and the attitude you have, but I need you to personally realize that all of us are equally special to the patient in our own way. It's a team effort."

"I'm not sure I know what to do with that, Mel."

"It's not so much about doing; it's about how you show up at work and at home. I'm asking you to not put so much emphasis on our jobs—on you being a physician and me being a nurse. I'm asking you to realize that we both have the same role as far as the patient's concerned. Just take a little more time and come back to me when that makes sense to you."

She got up, gave him a peck on the cheek, and was out the door. He didn't know what to do except finish off the bottle of wine in front of him.

FORTY-THREE

The alarm clock sounded like an air-raid siren. Ben didn't know whether to get out of bed or take cover under it. It only took a millisecond for him to process the hotel room and Mel's absence.

Everything she had said last night made sense. She was right. Everything he did began and ended with him, with his survival and ascendency as a physician. But that's not why he became a physician to begin with. When did things change without him even realizing it?

Mel had been the second person this week to tell him how his home problems and work problems were connected—the difference being that Mel had no problem letting him know the source of his supposed troubles. But how could he do something substantive about it? Maybe Jack Martin could give him a nudge in the right direction.

FORTY-FOUR

With the third NEI meeting just days away, Jack felt pretty good about Jane Carolli's progress, but like her, he wouldn't mind having a few more allies going in. When his secretary announced that Dr. Ben Waller was waiting outside, he couldn't help but feel more optimistic.

"Ben, come on in. What can I do for you?"

"Jack, I was wondering if you had a few minutes to offer me a little advice?"

"Of course. Work or personal stuff?"

"That's the thing, Mel's got me convinced that everything's related and I'm really struggling with it. I get it and it makes sense, but I don't know what to do with it."

"Can you be more specific, Ben? What exactly are we talking about?"

"Mel made it perfectly clear that I don't look at us as equals. How could I? Yes, what she says makes sense to me, but I don't know how to process it— what to do with it. Medical school only confirmed that we physicians are not the same as everyone else. You know what it's like, Jack. The competition begins in college the second you make up your mind to go to medical school. Then it does nothing but intensify. People may think of the corporate world when they think of social Darwinism, but they've never been to medical school. And now, I find myself unable to fully trust or respect this woman, the only woman I've ever really wanted. I feel like I've changed so much over the last fifteen years and it's bothering me."

Jack sat and absorbed what Ben was saying before sharing. "Ben, you probably have changed a lot. We all have. It's normal. But it's a two-sided coin. It means we're just as capable of changing again."

"That's all well and good, Jack, but where do I begin?"

"Let's talk about the work side for a minute. What do you see, or does Mel see, as your biggest problem?"

"She thinks I want nothing more than to excel and build my practice, and that my fear of screwing up or getting on the wrong side of the Ethan Langs of this world guides a lot of my decision making. And of course, that I don't treat her like an equal."

"Is she right?"

"Yes."

"Good."

"Great, Jack. I just admitted to being a wimp and not giving my girlfriend what she needs and you think that's good?"

"I think it's good that you admitted it, yes. I think that you wouldn't have if you didn't want to change things."

"Fine. But what do I do about it?"

"First, you need to figure out what you really want."

That was a no-brainer. "I want it all, Jack. I want to move back into my house, I want mutual respect, and I want to practice good medicine without looking over my shoulder."

"Then just do it, Ben. But don't do it for Mel. Do it for yourself. Otherwise, you won't be able to hold yourself accountable."

"What do you mean?"

"I've got a little exercise we can do that will help you to better define where you are now, where you want to be, how you got to this point, and what you need to do to move forward. In fact, I'm using the same exercise with Jane Carolli."

"How do I start?"

"We need to set aside some time and I'll run through a few exercises with you. I've got a meeting in ten minutes, so let's schedule something for later in the week."

"Sure. That's fine. But is there anything I can do right now?"

"Tell her, Ben. Tell Melanie how you see yourself today and how you'd like to be. Tell her you're working on it. Tell yourself the truth, and then tell her."

FORTY-FIVE

Jack welcomed Jane into his office. Jane had promised she would come to him, in her attempt at leveling the playing field.

"So Jane, how goes the battle?"

"Pretty good, Jack. You've just given me so much to think about. I ask myself whether I am leading or managing about ten times a day. And since our last visit, I'm starting to think of myself as more of a coach than anything else."

"That's good, right?"

"Yes, it tells me that I'm looking at my world differently, which gives me realistic hope that changes are coming. I have about thirty minutes now. What do you have in mind for me?"

"I thought we'd better run through what I hope to share with the NEI group. I'm going to start with using the incident to frame a conversation about where we are today, how we got here, where we want to go, and how to get there."

"So everything we've been talking about so far, the job-role stuff and that negative cycle we've put ourselves in?"

"Yes, Jane. So with you today, I'd like to look a little more closely at it by breaking down our job description versus our role description."

"We all have different jobs, Jack. How can we come up with some kind of general language about jobs? It seems easier when we talk about our roles, because they're all the same. Right?"

"Absolutely. We all have the same role. Okay, then instead of thinking about what we all do in our jobs, there's another way to look at it. When you have to put together an evaluation, what criteria do you use to assess job performance?"

Jane pulled out a legal pad and started scribbling while Jack gave her the space to do so.

"Okay, first, I look at their skill levels—if they know their stuff, make informed decisions, and are consistently competent."

"Good. Let's try to categorize those. Are we talking about how well they do their job?"

"Yes, Jack, but more than that, it has to do with aptitude, capacity..."

"How about talent? I think that's what you're defining."

"Okay, I'll buy that. First I judge their talent."

"What else?"

Jane looked at her notes. "Well, they need to leverage their talent to get things done, to get results. They may have the talent, but without execution..."

"Okay, so we have talent and execution. Anything else?"

"As a manager, I look to see if they show up every day ready to go, but as a leader, I think of it more as going the extra mile. Are they truly dedicated?"

"Talent, execution, and dedication. Those are the three categories you use when you evaluate staff?"

"Pretty much. They all have different jobs, but I guess I do judge them by the same criteria. So if that's job criteria, what's their role truly about?"

"Think about it, Jane, in the context of everything we've talked about. If you evaluate a staff member according to your criteria, which I agree with by the way, you should be set, right?"

"Not really, Jack. Even if they score high, that doesn't mean they'll be any easier to work with. Lang may score well on an evaluation, but he still works solo and is a complete pain in the ass."

"Okay, then what do we want from him, from everyone?"

"Well, if I use Lang as an example, I'd have to start with playing well with others as first on the list."

Jack pulled up his pad. "Okay, first, is the person a team player?"

"I don't know, Jack, how can Lang become a team player when he's so unapproachable? Everyone is afraid to talk to him, much less be in the same room with him."

"So you're saying that people need to feel safe when they approach him."

Jane quickly added, "And that will only happen if the guy actually values what someone other than himself has to say."

"Agreed. In a word, all of us have to convey that we're 'Safe to Approach.' That's second after Team Player on our role description list. What's next?"

"Before Lang or anyone can value our opinions, they have to listen. And I mean really listen, Jack. It's so easy to judge what people are saying before they even finish their thoughts. We need to–I need to–hear people out and frame everything they have to say in a positive way, even if I disagree with them. It seems like we're predisposed to thinking negatively first. What's that about?"

"You're right, Jane, it's probably a protective mechanism, a direct result of the competition and high stakes inherent in healthcare."

"You would think 'Understanding' wouldn't be so hard to come by in the profession of saving lives."

"Go figure. Okay, Jane, we have 'Team Player, Safe to Approach, and Understanding.' Anything else?"

"I know I'm missing something, but I'm not sure what, Jack."

"Think about Ethan Lang—since he's a good example of how we don't want to show up."

"He treats me, he treats everyone, with such contempt and disrespect. How can anyone feel valued around him?"

"Perfect. Number four is 'Respect.'"

"Yep, you have that right. A little respect would go a long way around here."

"Is that it?"

Jane looked down at her pad and said, "I think so. Oh yeah, and showing up like a coach would be icing on the cake. So what do you think, Jack?"

"Team Player, Safe to Approach, Respectful, and Understanding. Sounds about right. The big four."

"Add those to my evaluation criteria, and I'd have the perfect staff."

Jane sat for a minute, obviously lost in thought.

"Jack, when I think about the big four, it's kind of ridiculous that all of this didn't occur to me sooner. I mean, these are the basics we're looking for when building friendships, partners...they're the things you need to really work well together with someone. I just didn't think of it as something I should be concerned about as a leader. I mean, coming up with an agreement like we did."

Jack said, "A pact."

"Yes, a pact, that's just the beginning. You're telling me that this way of structuring relationships begins with the coaching relationship. And I need to be intentional about using these pacts with my entire leadership team, and eventually with everyone."

"You nailed it, Jane. Coaching your way to a more productive patient-centered relationship is a primary leadership competency. These pacts have to become part of your go-to tools."

Jane broke in, "Maybe the most important leadership tool. I mean, if we're really going to be a patient-centered hospital, then we have to structure relationships based on the big four behaviors. That's really what being patient-centered is all about, isn't it?"

"Definitely," said Jack. "In fact, you and I should probably redo our pact. I need to be even more deliberate about how I approach relationships, all relationships."

"Because the better you are at structuring relationships, the less you leave patient care to chance. In fact, we need to weave structuring relationships into all of our business practices. Whether we're hiring, evaluating, having a meeting, or in the OR, a successful outcome for our patients depends on this."

"Right, Jane, because an effective leader leaves as little to chance as possible."

"Okay, I get it, Jack. But what's the end game here? If I, as a leader, treat building patient-centered relationships as a priority, aren't I trying to change the whole culture? That sounds so big and unreachable, but that's where this is going, isn't it?"

"It only sounds big if you think of it in those terms. But as you already know, it begins small, one-to-one, and continues to build that way. It's not so unreachable-sounding when you think of it that way."

"I hear you. Everybody's always throwing the word 'culture' around to the point of it having very little meaning. But this is an actual, concrete way of making a cultural shift."

"A cultural shift that you can engineer, Jane. And it all begins with these patient-centered pacts...these contracts."

"It's funny, Jack, I deal with contracts every day. But they're usually a hundred pages long and most of the pages are about protecting ourselves from each other."

Jack smiled. "And why's that?"

Jane didn't hesitate. "Because we've always based everything on the same criteria...on talent, getting things done, and work ethic. We never even considered teamwork, being safe to approach, respect, and understanding. If we incorporated these values into our contracts, we could really cut them down to size. We need to think less about our job differences and more about the similar role we have for our patients."

"Wouldn't that make us all more accountable to each other?"

"Yes," said Jane. "That's exactly what our patients need."

Jack added, "Our patients just want to believe that they're getting the best care possible, and that means feeling like they're on the same page as we are, not on a different planet than we are. They want to at least feel like they're a part of our team. And it begins with everyone seeing us coaching each other, not ignoring and belittling each other."

Jane sat there overwhelmed in a good way for a change. For the first time in her tenure as head honcho she realized the difference between managing and leading, and the importance of being a coach to her team, and was chomping at the bit to get this thing moving forward.

"Thanks, Jack. What's our next step?"

"I think we should talk about how we can begin sharing what we know with our captive audience in the next NEI meeting. Why don't you join me on rounds and we'll talk about it."

"You don't have any patients of your own, Jack. What gives?"

"Don't you go on rounds, Jane?"

"Well I used to as a nurse, of course, and I know some managers have. But besides the fact that I don't have time for it, I'm not sure what to say. Funny enough, even after half a lifetime working with patients, it's a little out of my comfort zone."

"All that I can tell you, Jane, is that everything we're talking about began with performing rounds in Billings when I didn't have any patients. At first, I started asking them what kind of improvement they'd like to see—big mistake. I already knew the answer and every conversation started off negatively. Then, I asked them what was really important to them, and I got an entirely new perspective, something I could really use. Although patients framed their answers differently, they all essentially said the same thing."

"They were saying that they wanted to trust their caregivers?"

"Not in those specific terms, but yes, they were all alluding to something relational instead of physical. They all had their own hierarchy of concerns, and everything funneled down to trusting that we were all truly listening to them and hiding nothing from them. Like you just said, they want to feel engaged in a team effort to make them better."

Jane smiled. "So basically, the patients are looking for the same things we need from each other—the ability to put all of our past stuff aside and work together."

"Bingo."

"In fact, Jane, once I figured it out, and things began to improve, I looked forward to doing rounds more than anything else. When the improved workforce started taking shape, the patients started raving about the care. I realized that if I needed a pat on the back, I'd get it from rounding. Sold yet?"

As she rose and headed for the door she said, "Yep, I'll be there."

FORTY-SIX

Life seemed pretty good to Ben, or at least better. Mel believed him when he told her about his newfound perspective, because it was the truth. They talked all night long about how he had reached his recent epiphanies and how he would handle things from here on out.

He'd been living in a fear-driven world that he created himself, and he'd lost the ability to trust. In retrospect, it all made sense. Pre-med was nothing if not competitive, and medical school, internship, and residency were all about leaving your fellow students in the dust and doing whatever it took to best position yourself for success.

When he started at Angels, he believed that success would only come if he followed Ethan Lang's lead, and maybe it still did, but it wasn't worth it if it was going to cost one more life, or his relationship with Mel.

The night before, when Mel asked him when he had last thought of Edie, it was like a slap in the face. He hadn't thought about her at all lately. That wouldn't happen again. Granted, he couldn't keep the memory of every one of his patients alive and present twenty-four/seven, but he now knew that Edie and the Edies of the future were the reason why he came to work every day, and he wouldn't lose sight of that ever again.

He didn't even see or hear Dr. Lang when he walked into the locker room.

"Waller." Again. "Waller, are you sleepwalking or what?"

"Sorry, Dr. Lang, just lost in thought." *Damn,* he thought, *I have to stop being so apologetic.*

Ben continued, "I was just thinking about Edie. When's the last time you gave her some thought?"

"Who the hell is Edie?"

"She's the reason we're having these Never Event Investigation meetings.

The person who died because we didn't have the capacity to work well together."

With a little Groucho Marx in his tone, Lang snapped, "Waller, why don't you bore a hole in yourself and let the sap run out? If you let every little setback slow you down, you won't last in this business. Do I wish she hadn't died? Of course. But it happens."

"But we caused it. We could've kept it from happening."

"You're an idiot if you believe that."

"No disrespect, Dr. Lang, but if Dr. Hartley had listened to his transcriptionist or if you had given Julie, the OR nurse, five seconds to check out the scan, Edie would probably be fine."

"Who the hell do you think you're talking to?"

"I guess I'm still trying to figure that out. Please, indulge me for a moment."

Lang started to head for the door. "Give me one reason why I should."

"Because I've been a good referrer, I've done everything you've ever asked of me, and I'm a fellow physician asking for your help."

"That's how you ask for someone's help—by pointing fingers at him?"

"You're right. That was the wrong approach. But can you tell me that I was completely wrong?"

"It's more complicated than that, Waller. I can't possibly know about the dynamics between Hartley and his staff, and I've been going by his and other physician's notes and corresponding body markings for thirty years. And this never happened before. It was an anomaly, nothing more."

"I have to disagree. It may be a first for you. But it was still a fatal decision for Edie and her family. Isn't it true that you didn't look at the scan because Julie was just a young nurse and you didn't trust her?"

"Why the hell should I trust her, you, or anyone around here? If I want something done right, I know I'd better do it myself."

"But what if we did respect each other a little bit more? You might have looked at the scan."

"What's gotten into you? Have you been drinking Jack Martin's Kool-Aid? That guy may have had some success in backwater Montana, but this is the real world. We don't have time to stand in a circle, hold hands and sing together every time we need to make a quick decision."

"But what if we just took ten seconds before we made a decision, especially one that holds a life in the balance? Don't you think there's any value in us working as a team?"

Ethan Lang just stared at him for a few seconds (talk about irony) and then said, "I know that the third NEI is coming up in a day or two. Do you know something I don't? Because it sounds like you're looking to make Hartley and me the scapegoats here."

"No, Dr. Lang. It's bigger than the two of you and all of us in that meeting. It's systemic. I just think we should look at this as an opportunity to work together better, to improve."

He turned his back and walked through the door while saying, "You've used enough of my time."

FORTY-SEVEN

Ethan Lang made a beeline for Jane Carolli's office to see if Waller's line of questioning came from his chronic naïveté, or was a result of some kind of ploy to put that girl's death on him and Hartley.

He was a little taken aback that Waller had actually stood up to him. Maybe he had backbone after all. But backbone or not, there was a hierarchy around here and physicians had to look after each other. You would think he'd have figured it out by now.

Lang bullied his way through Carolli's outer office and pushed open the inner office door without acknowledging her secretary's presence, much less her questions.

On her way out the door, Jane collided with Lang, nearly lost her balance, and just caught herself before hitting the deck.

"What the hell, Dr. Lang, haven't you heard of knocking, or for that matter checking in with my secretary instead of nearly clotheslining me?"

"Sorry about that—I'm going to be late for rounds and I needed a minute of your time beforehand."

She was about to say that she was headed for rounds too, but caught herself before getting stuck with the task of trying to justify what she was doing.

"Well, Ethan, you're aptly blocking my escape route, so what can I do for you?"

"Look, I'm not blind, Jane, I know that you brought Dr. Martin in to stir things up here, but I didn't realize how much until I just got reamed out by Dr. Waller."

Jane could barely contain her excitement at the thought of another ally onboard! Calmly she continued, "Reamed out? What do you mean?"

"He practically blamed Dr. Hartley and me for that girl's death and gave me the impression that you'd be pointing the finger at us during the next NEI meeting."

"I can assure you Dr. Lang, that's not the case..."

He interrupted, "It better not be, because I can tell you right now, although I don't want to get confrontational, if I feel like I'm being attacked, I will respond with the entire Medical Executive Committee at my side. And you can ask your predecessor how that went for him."

Pause, Jane, pause, she said to herself.

In the kindest possible tone she could manage, she said, "I really can't believe Dr. Waller was threatening you at all. Threats are very uncomfortable for me, and I wouldn't, or I should say, won't let them become a tactic around here. Do we understand each other?"

Before he could answer she continued, "Drs. Waller, Martin, and I are putting our heads together to improve how we all work together around here. I've decided to try to make something good come out of these NEI meetings. To use them as an opportunity to find some common ground and figure out a way for Edie's loss to bring about some positive change."

He began to talk and she cut him off, "And we want you and everyone at that meeting to work with us. That's what the next meeting will cover. It's not about you, Hartley, or any one person, but about why things happened and how we can move forward to get physicians, nurses, and administrators on the same page working together. We need to learn to listen and respect each other or the patients will never be able to trust us."

Ethan Lang didn't know how to respond. For the second time in an hour, someone he had confronted didn't back down. And for some reason he wasn't sure of yet, he found himself at a loss for words. As long as they weren't pointing the finger at him or Simon Hartley, he really didn't have a lot of ground to stand on. But he also knew that he wouldn't be taking the word of a "wet behind the ears" nurse over his own instincts. This Edie person was a tragedy, but an anomaly for sure. Never happened before and never will again. At least not to him.

Fine, he thought to himself, *I'll let them play with their ideas, but if one hint of blame comes our way at the meeting, she'll learn the meaning of "No Confidence Vote" and be out the door before she even knows it hit her on the ass.*

"Okay, Jane, I believe you. You play your useless exercises and waste all the time you want, you're the boss...just leave me out of it."

"I'd rather have you joining in, Ethan. You're the most experienced and skilled physician we have; it would mean a lot to the process if we had your buy-in."

"Just enjoy the fact that I'm giving you this much rope. As long as it doesn't effect me, like I said, I'll leave you to it."

When Jane heard the "rope" comment she could feel the steam starting to build, but she didn't act on it. She realized that there are times to draw a line in the sand and times to wait. She would wait. But she couldn't help giving him her most defiant look.

Lang saw Carolli back off, but not down. He knew he had to rally the troops before the next NEI happened. As he barreled out the door, he was already on his cell phone setting up the second impromptu meeting of the MEC in a month.

FORTY-EIGHT

Jane headed out onto the third floor to reconnoiter with Jack Martin. She felt almost giddy at the thought of engaging patients again and wondered why it had taken all this time, and a vice president for Medical Affairs from Montana, to get her back into the trenches.

She just didn't know where to start or what to say, which is why she felt a sense of relief when Jack turned the corner.

"Good news, Jack, I just quelled a mini-tirade from Ethan Lang about a run-in he had with Ben Waller."

"I guess that's good."

"Well, actually it was, because I handled him calmly, but that's not the only upside. He complained about Waller, because Waller questioned him about Edie and the purpose of the next NEI meeting. Of course, Lang took it as a threat. But the real news is that Ben Waller stood up to him—he seems to have turned a corner. You must have reached him."

"I think it was probably more about Ms. Swift getting his attention, but all the same, this is how it works, Jane. It starts with two, then a couple more."

"You know, Jack, I've been concentrating on how long it would take for this new approach to take root, instead of focusing on the small successes and the realization that it's going to take a while to turn this big ship around. But as more get onboard, things will speed up. I just need to keep living this thing and open the door to others."

"Yeah, Jane, it's not like you can throw a new initiative into a binder and expect everyone to follow it to a T. We already know how that works. As a leader, remember, the best contribution you can make is to become a coach so that you can help others to realize that no matter how different our jobs are, we all play the same role here."

When they turned the corner it was clear Jack was headed for one particular room.

"Jack, before we go in, I'm not sure what I should talk about."

"First off, it's more about asking something and spending most of the time listening. If we're going to give these patients what they need the most, we have to listen."

Almost to herself, she said, "Sounds like making a basic diagnosis."

"So what do you think you should ask, Jane?"

"Well, what if I ask them how we could improve their stay?"

"You tell me, Jane—is that something that you don't already know? Will that yield deeper insights into what we're trying to validate?"

"No."

Jack let her think for a moment and then said, "You mentioned making a basic diagnosis. This is a lot like that. Because the only way to really get to a more patient-centered approach is knowing how to ask the right questions. What do you want to know from them?"

"I guess I want to know what's most important to them—what really matters to them."

"There you go."

They continued on toward the room and Jack shared, "We're visiting Bill Meyers, a fifty-six-year-old male scheduled for a coronary angioplasty first thing tomorrow morning."

They walked into the room and Bill Meyers was facing the TV, but you could tell he wasn't really paying any attention to it. He almost snapped to attention when a new physician and a suit entered the room.

"Hi, what's going on—is anything wrong?"

Jane said, "No, Mr. Meyers, we're just stopping by for a visit. I'm Jane Carolli, I kind of run things around here, and this is Dr. Jack Martin—he's in charge of Medical Affairs. We just wanted to check in and see how you're doing."

"Wow, is this SOP? Oh, excuse the acronym, you can take the man out of the Marines, but not the other way around...is this standard operating procedure?"

"Well, yes and no," Jane answered. "We like to get out and visit with as many people as we can, when time permits."

"What can I help you with, Miss...?"

"Jane. It's the other way around, Mr. Meyers. You're the one who can help us. I just want to know more about what everyone's thinking around here. Tell me, what's the most important thing on your mind right now?"

"You mean besides getting out of here in one piece?"

"I mean, is there anything in particular that you're thinking about? Anything that would reassure you that you'll get out of here in one piece?"

"Well, there are a lot of people going in and out of this room and I can't help wondering if they're even talking to each other. It seems like twenty different bodies ask me the same question all day long, like one hand doesn't know what the other's doing. I mean no disrespect, but you hear about people getting the wrong meds and such, and it sure would be nice to know that everyone's on the same page, that people are actually talking to each other about me. Having my heart worked on is stressful enough if you know what I mean."

"I do," said Jane, "is there something you'd specifically like to see or hear?"

"I don't know." He stared right through the TV again for a minute. "I guess seeing more interaction would be nice...but I also realize there's probably all of that going on behind the curtain and I'm just not seeing it. I just want to believe it is. It would be nice to feel more confident about everything. I mean, not about my doc, or each of the nurses, just about everyone combined."

"This is why I'm here, Mr. Meyers..."

"Bill."

"Bill. I need to hear this from you so that I can figure new ways of making sure you get the peace of mind you deserve."

"Or at least some peace of mind," he countered. "Until they've been in and out of my arteries, it's hard to relax. But it sure would help if it felt like all of these people were on some kind of team."

"Let me see what I can do about that." Jane glanced back at Jack. "And I'll stop by tomorrow after your procedure and check in. I'll also stop by the nurses' station right now, and double check everything for you. I was a nurse and nurse manager, and I know there is a lot going on behind the curtain, as you said, but I also know that you shouldn't have to wonder about these kinds of things."

"Thank you."

"My pleasure, Bill. See you in the morning."

They had barely cleared the threshold when Jack asked, "What do you think?"

"I think he's really scared and some of his fears can be allayed, should be allayed by us."

Jack let it sink in for Jane as she stopped by the nurses' station and looked at Bill's chart. After confirming that everything looked good, they headed to the next room.

"You know, Jack, I'm looking forward to the next visit, and I don't know exactly what we'll be hearing, but I'll bet it will come down to the same thing Bill Meyers wants—to just trust that everyone's working together on his behalf."

"And the best way to ensure that, Jane, is adhering to what we talked about before we came into the room: becoming a coach."

Jane smiled. "Yeah, Jack, I get it. This is going to be a part of my daily practice. Maybe not every day, but as often as I can."

She paused a few seconds. "I always thought that I knew what being patient-centered was, but I didn't. If we can get someone like Mr. Meyers to trust that all of us are truly working together on his behalf, then we'll really be patient-centered."

"Well said. But don't beat yourself up over it. I'll bet everyone in this hospital has a different definition, and it's not that they're all wrong. I guess I just look at it a little differently."

FORTY-NINE

alling an unscheduled MEC meeting at day's end was not the norm, and not telling Jane Carolli about it...that was definitely out of the ordinary. And calling two such unscheduled meetings in a month's time might be construed as desperate. *But desperate measures for desperate times,* thought Ethan Lang as he rounded the hall toward conference room 2B. He couldn't stop thinking that no matter what Carolli or Waller said, he and Hartley were in the crosshairs, while all he had done was spend the last thirty-two years saving lives and making people well. He had worked like a dog to become one of the top surgeons in the city, and some new cowboy and his chemistry set experiments weren't going to tarnish his career one iota. He thought, *Nothing good has come from Jack Martin joining our staff.*

He needed to raise the White Wall and get the MEC members started on devising a strategy to get Martin out of this hospital. And if Jane Carolli wanted to hitch her wagon to him, they could both ride off into the sunset together.

When Ethan Lang entered the conference room he was taken aback to see a couple of chairs empty. He knew it was a last-minute meeting, but he needed and expected everyone's support. Dr. Hunnywell from Emergency was missing, along with Simms from Gastroenterology. He noticed Waller had showed up—he would deal with him later. For now, Lang had neither the patience nor the time to wait.

"Okay, everyone, settle down. I know this is last minute, but I needed this meeting to happen before tomorrow's third NEI meeting concerning the death of..." he looked down at his notes, "Edie Worden. And since it's been a long day for all of us, we're not going to approve any minutes or deal with any credential work...or any new items for that matter. We're here partly because I'm pretty sure this hospital blames Simon Hartley and me for this Worden issue. Of course, I can't be too worried about it because we're insured, we weren't to blame, and this institution is just as liable as we are..."

Dr. Bill Proctor from Radiology interrupted, "Come on, Ethan, we know this won't end up on you. Why are we here?"

If looks could kill. Lang continued, "All right, Bill, everyone, I want to gather some consensus on what the new vice president for Medical Affairs is trying to do...with Jane Carolli's support I might add, and why we need to start thinking of replacing him."

Dave Lee spoke up, "But he just got here, Ethan. What could he have possibly done to make you want to get so drastic so fast?"

"Look," said Lang, "this guy wants Carolli to completely change how we work around here. He wants to make us accountable to nurses and force us to make our decisions by consensus...and if that's not enough..."

"Excuse me, Dr. Lang," said Ben Waller, "but I'm pretty sure that's not what his intent is at all. He's just talking about all of us being better listeners and respecting each other's experience and working more like teams on behalf of our patients."

"Believe what you want, Waller. This guy thinks if we play nice with each other, accidents won't happen, and everything will be hunky-dory."

Ben wanted to say something about the fact that Lang was pretty much admitting that an accident did happen on his watch, but instead, he answered, "I think that he's saying if we listened to people better and took a few seconds before making decisions, things might have ended differently in Edie's case... and others."

Seemingly emboldened, Simon Hartley spoke up, "Ethan, if I had listened to that transcriptionist better, maybe..."

Lang cut him off, "It wasn't your fault, Simon, or mine. It just happened. Are you ready for everything to change around here...are you ready to make decisions by consensus?"

"No, I'm not. If that is indeed the case, I am not. To be honest, I'm a short timer; my career is almost over. I have no desire to make any changes to how I work. As far as I'm concerned, you can put a fork in me, I'm done and almost out."

It wasn't exactly the ringing endorsement Ethan Lang wanted, but at least

Simon wasn't willing to go along for the ride.

Lang continued, "Look, I just wanted to let you know what I see coming down the pike, and it's not good for physicians. Already, almost half of the physicians in this hospital have given up their autonomy and joined the organization. Now it feels like the organization wants us to get approval from everyone else in the room before we make decisions. If that's what you want then do nothing. But if you like things how they are...if you want to continue to be respected as the captains of this ship, then let's start thinking about how to strategically remove Dr. Jack Martin."

Ben Waller had his second epiphany in a week. He stood up and said, "Dr. Lang, you're a fine surgeon and you have helped my career a lot. But I'm having a real problem with your logic here. First, I've never heard Jack Martin or Jane Carolli ever say anything about making decisions by consensus... nor do they want to take away our autonomy. They just want us to work better together on behalf of our patients. And second, I've decided to let go of my practice and work for the hospital. Not because anyone pressured me in this direction, but because in my case, it will eliminate a lot of the business side and tedium of running my own practice, and allow me to better concentrate on my patients."

Ben sat down feeling a little dizzy again, but this time in a good way...like the buzz of having a glass or two of champagne.

Dr. Ethan Lang had no immediate comeback for Ben. He shook his head and said, "All of you do what you want, but if you want my support, and you want to keep control of the way you practice medicine, you'll work with me to proactively stop Jack Martin from pushing his ideas down our throats. That's all I have. Meeting adjourned."

FIFTY

Ben opened his eyes to Mel's empty side of the bed. He sat bolt upright, looking around for her, when he heard her voice from the kitchen, "Relax, big guy, I'm here, just getting the coffee going."

He dropped back down, relieved. Not only because they were together, but for how he was beginning to feel so grounded, something he never really felt before.

"Today's the NEI, Mel. It ought to be fun. After all the mutiny Lang experienced last night, Jack's going to have his hands full with Lang."

She walked into the room carrying a tray with a full bistro of coffee, cups, and toasted English Muffins.

Smiling, she said, "I just can't get over how proud I am of you, and how excited I am that you're going to work for the hospital. No more office worries or referral worries. And no more kowtowing to Lang."

"I've got to think, Mel, that even if I showed up every day and kissed his feet, Lang would never forgive me for my stance last night."

"He's a great physician, Ben, but he's a dinosaur and his ego had a lot to do with Edie dying. And you don't need him."

Ben repeated, "Jack's sure going to have his hands full with him today."

"But he won't be alone, Ben."

"That's true," said Ben, "Carolli will be there."

"And so will we."

"I know, I know. Don't worry. I really do feel good about the way things are going. I'm not going to sit there with my mouth shut if I have something to say. I proved that yesterday."

She settled down next to him. "I know. I'm so happy for you Ben...for us. Now make yourself useful and pour me a cuppa joe."

FIFTY-ONE

NEVER EVENT INVESTIGATION III

When Jack and Jane entered the meeting room, they could feel the "uncomfortable" oozing their way. Lang, Hartley, and Zeller pretended to talk golf, Julie looked blank-faced, while Mel stared and smiled at Ben, who looked like the reborn picture of confidence. The group left the two heads of the table open for the perceived purveyors of doom and gloom.

Jack didn't waste any time. "Thank you all for coming. I want to set the tone up front so that everyone feels clear about why we're here and what we're after. Notice I said we, because we need to gravitate closer to the same page today, and learn how to avoid repeating the mistakes we made with Edie."

Lang pounced, "If you're talking about us physicians, Dr. Martin, just come out with it, if you're really going to be up front."

Jack paused a few seconds to let the sting of his tone evaporate.

"You're absolutely right, Dr. Lang. I'll make it crystal clear. I'm not on a witch hunt for you or anyone. We're here to have a conversation about what matters most to patients. We're having these NEIs because we failed Edie, and we need to work together to ensure that doesn't happen again."

Dr. Hartley, seemingly emboldened by his proximity to Lang, added, "Sure, we can have a conversation, but what good is talking when we obviously need something more concrete for the nurses to follow, some kind of a checklist?"

Mel told herself to not react emotionally, but seeing Julie cringe next to her, she said, "Excuse me, Dr. Hartley, but Dr. Martin specifically said this wasn't about blame, so why don't we all try not to go down that road?"

"Sure, Ms. Swift," added Lang, "as long as that applies to you too."

"You know me, Dr. Lang, I always do what I'm told, and..."

Jack interrupted, "Melanie, do you know what the definition of sarcasm is?"

Taken aback, she answered, "Dr. Martin, that's just my sense of humor."

"I get it, but it's also a way to mask contempt, frequently at someone else's expense...which flies in the face of everything we're going to try to accomplish today."

Jack paused for a minute.

"Melanie, I didn't mean to jump on you, but you hit a nerve and brought me back to the way I used to be. Sarcasm came easy to me, and I still have to work on keeping it at bay. It took me most of my life, but I finally realized that no matter how innocuous an attempt at humor is, all it does is stand in the way of the positive tone we need...that our patients need. So let's all of us drop our snarky attitudes and try to remember that we're here because a young woman is dead and we could've prevented it."

"Fine, Dr. Martin," said Lang, facing Jane Carolli, "as long as we're all held to the same standard."

Jack didn't give Jane time to reply. "Yes, Dr. Lang, we are. But tell me, in your OR, who's at the top? Who's the captain of the ship in there?"

"Of course, it's me. Who else?"

"Isn't it the captain's responsibility to set the tone in the OR?"

"Of course," said Lang, unsure of where Martin was headed.

"Then Dr. Lang, what kind of tone did you set that morning?"

"Well, that's easy. I was professional, thorough as always, and ready to give my best."

"And is that the tone you feel like you're setting now?"

"You must be kidding me, Dr. Martin. Are you comparing behavior in a meeting room to how we perform in surgery?"

"I am."

"That's ridiculous."

Dr. Zeller broke in, "What do you mean by that, Jack?"

Jack answered, "I just said that WE could have prevented this. It didn't happen because of any one person's mistake, but because the current culture here at Angels doesn't encourage teamwork. Look, we work in a culture that doesn't hold its people accountable to group problem-solving. And for that matter, the rest of the healthcare world doesn't either."

Jack Martin let everyone think about that for a second, caught a support-ive glance from Jane, and began again.

"First, whether we're in a meeting or surgery, don't you agree we need to start being respectful of what everyone says, and be responsive to their needs. Can't you see that's the only way to build truly functioning teams?"

"That's all good and fine on paper, Martin," barked Lang, "but this senti-mental stuff isn't going to save anyone's life. Good cutting is."

Ben Waller blurted out, "Don't you think some teamwork around here would be a good thing, Dr. Lang? And starting by being respectful makes sense."

"I get that, Waller. But I'd rather have someone cutting on me who has experience and knows his stuff than just a nice respectful guy who listens to my problems."

Ben defiantly said, "Can't we be both? Look, everyone screwed up. I was in the gallery during the original incident and I didn't speak up. I'd told myself it was because I wasn't in there…wasn't privy to the charts…when really I was just making excuses to myself to cover for a fellow physician. I wasn't basing my actions on what mattered most to Edie at the time. And I wasn't being a team player…supporting my team for the sake and welfare of the patient. I still beat myself up over it, but I guarantee you, it will never happen again."

Melanie beamed with admiration, and Jane Carolli took it in, deciding not to respond and affect the flow of conversation surrounding Dr. Lang.

Jack let Ben's comment hang for a second and pressed on. "Dr. Lang, I'm not saying you have to admire or even like everyone you work with, but you'll be doing yourself and the patient a huge disservice if you don't have enough regard for their abilities and experience to really listen to what they have to say."

"After all," Jane interjected, "none of us as individuals is smarter than all the brains in the room combined."

As Carolli tag-teamed with Dr. Martin, she seemed different to Melanie. Melanie couldn't put a label on it, but she seemed to radiate renewed confi-dence. And she wore it really well.

Jack said, "Look, we really need to be more understanding when it comes to listening without judgment. It's the only way we'll ever learn anything new. And is there anyone in this room who feels like they have nothing left to learn?"

He let that sink in.

"Next, we need to change this place into a safe place to work."

Dr. Zeller inquired, "What do you mean by safe?"

"Thanks for asking, Doctor. I mean a place that fosters safe exchanges of opinions or ideas. A place where a nurse, or a tech for that matter, knows that they can add something to a conversation that needs adding, without fear of retribution or scorn."

Ethan Lang couldn't contain himself, "Are you suggesting we physicians start making decisions after letting everyone weigh in...make decisions by consensus? Because that's not only the craziest idea ever—it will end up delaying care and mistreating patients."

Jack continued, "I never said anything like that nor would I ever want that. I'm simply saying that if we all start to make this place safe and respectful, we'll set the stage for actually working in teams. Because if we can't be team players, then we won't give patients what they need the most, to trust that they're in the right place, that they have the right physicians and nurses, and that everyone communicates with each other on their behalf. They really need to trust we're all on the same page, on the same team."

"Look, Martin," said Lang, "you're fooling yourself. All the patients want is to recover and get out of here alive. Trust has nothing to do with it. It's all about clinical excellence."

Jane jumped in, "I'd like to share something that happened to me this week that addresses what's being said here. I started rounding for the first time since I took over as CEO. I couldn't believe I hadn't done it before, and realized that if I want to truly become patient-centered, I'd better talk to the patients. Although they all had different concerns, everything came down to trust."

She continued, "Let me explain. The first patient I talked with, Bill, a fifty-six-year-old, retired full-bird marine colonel, was scheduled for a coronary angioplasty first thing the next morning. And 'jarhead' or not, he was as white as a sheet when I walked through the door. I asked him what the most important thing on his mind was, and he said that he couldn't believe how many people asked him the same questions over the course of the day. He felt like the right hand didn't know what the left was doing."

Melanie jumped in, "That's pretty normal, Ms. Carolli—I mean, all of us want to make sure we know where the patient stands."

"I know, Melanie, but this patient wants to know that we talk to each other so he doesn't feel compelled to double-check medications and such himself. He wants to trust that we communicate. He just plain wants to put his trust in us."

Ben chimed in, "I agree, Dr. Lang, that above all, they want to get out of here in one piece, but part of making that happen depends on their state of mind while they're here. If we give them what they need, our jobs become easier by making them more responsive to what we ask of them."

Ethan Lang just sat there looking like he was chewing on nails.

Jack took over, "Think about what we've talked through so far. Think about being respectful, understanding, and creating a safe place to talk, and working together in teams. And think about what the colonel wanted. Then think back to the morning of Edie's surgery. This isn't about blame, but what would have happened if we had operated as a team in that safe place I just described? Would the outcome have been different?"

"Obviously," said Julie, speaking up for the first time. "Everything would have been different."

Zeller said, "But you're talking about the best possible situation. How do you expect us to get there from here?"

Lang looked disgustedly at Zeller but didn't utter a word.

"Yes," agreed Dr. Hartley, "it all sounds unattainable. Although, if I'd been thinking this way when I blew up at my transcriptionist..." he said shaking his head sideways and looking down at the floor.

"Dammit, Simon," screeched Lang, "this wasn't your fault."

Trying to stop blood pressures from rising, Jack quickly added, "This isn't about one particular event, Dr. Hartley. As I said earlier, we just weren't trained this way. And I agree with you, it sounds challenging, but why not work toward the best possible outcome?"

"I know one thing," added Melanie, "if we don't figure out where we want to go, we're never going to get there. And nothing bad ever comes out of setting the bar high. This sounds pretty tangible. If we can create checklists, why can't we create some kind of personal code type of checklist?"

Jane Carolli smiled, saying, "We can, Melanie."

Then she engaged Ethan Lang with a calmness none of them had ever seen before.

"Ethan, Dr. Martin asked us to think about how the outcome with Edie would have been different that morning if the OR had been a safe place that encouraged everyone's contribution. Let me ask you this, what if it was your mother having the lobectomy that morning? Would you rather have been working in the culture we're describing?"

"You're asking me if I'd have taken the five seconds to look at the scan if it was my mother on the table?"

Jane hesitated for a few moments, not because all eyes were on her, but because she really wanted what she was about to say to come out right.

"No, Ethan. I don't need to ask you a question we all know the answer to, because we are all products of the same system and more alike than we might want to admit. And we were never trained to create a safe, respectful atmosphere. If we all had your skills and track record, we'd have probably done what you did. And I know for sure that we all would have checked the scan if our own mothers were on the table."

Dr. Ethan Lang didn't pounce, but he still looked like he had a mouthful of tenpenny nails.

Again, Melanie was impressed with Jane Carolli's tone. She didn't sound like a leader when she talked to Lang...more like a coach. Her voice and tone lacked confrontation. If anything, she was more encouraging and positive.

Jack jumped right back in, "You see, what happened to Edie doesn't fall on individual physicians or nurses, but the best way to avoid it happening again is for us to create the right conditions for teamwork."

Jane added, "Look, I may be Dr. Martin's boss, but he's been coaching me since his arrival. And it's become very clear that coaching—or interacting with each other as coaches instead of like leaders and subordinates—is the primary component needed to build a team that really works. And that's what our patients expect from us. So the bottom line is that we need to start thinking of ourselves as coaches."

"Thanks, Jane," said Jack. "And as weird as it sounds, none of us has been trained how to build teams or coach. Our education has emphasized the skills needed to do our jobs, not the behaviors needed to get us working together. Hell, we don't even know how to leverage one-to-one relationships. How should we be expected to work as teams in the first place?"

Jack continued, "But we're the only ones who can change things for the better and keep this from happening again. First one-to-one, then in small groups like this, and then, eventually, we can take it viral throughout the hospital."

Jack continued, "Answer me this, what's the connection between how we showed up that day and what we got in the end?"

Ben said, "The fact that we're having this meeting pretty much sums up what could have been avoided. What a concept. What if instead of worrying about who's going to end up under the bus, we were more focused on working together? As soon as this thing went down, all I could think about was my career."

"That's the only thing you should have been thinking about," said Lang, "and I did the same thing. We physicians have to take care of our own. But you obviously don't get that, Waller."

Jane Carolli realized at that point that Ethan Lang wasn't about to change his ways. He was going to fight this all the way until he retired. A month ago she would have felt pretty threatened by the thought of it. Today, she could only think about how to hasten his departure and move forward without him.

Again trying to de-fuse the situation, Jack said, "Ben, what's the value in any of us beating ourselves up over past behaviors, especially when we really had no frame of reference to begin with?"

"Tell me something, everyone," Jack continued. "If you could have done one thing different that day, what would it have been?"

Dr. Zeller shook his head with resignation, saying, "I could've been more forceful. I admit, before today, I've always been better at listening to physicians over nurses. I was the other physician in the room. I could have pushed it. Sorry, Ethan."

Ethan Lang knew that he'd been set up—this was where he was supposed to say that he was sorry to the nurse and that he should have looked at the scan. Instead, he just sat there.

Julie said, "I could've been more forceful too. I was just scared. I could've asked Dr. Zeller to take a look. Heck, I could've interrupted or interfered with the procedure and risked my job. I would've done that if it was my mother on the table."

"Remember what Dr. Martin just said," added Carolli. "This isn't about beating ourselves up, it's about moving forward."

Mel sat quietly, absorbing everything. Then she said, to no one in particular, "I never thought of myself as a checklist or a safeguard before, but when you think about it in the context of how we should be working more as a team, if just one of us had spoken up..."

Ben added, "Which means if all of us were onboard, it could prevent this from ever happening again. It would be like having a redundant protective system always in place."

"Yes, Ben," said Jane. "Like Dr. Martin said at the beginning of this meeting, it was never about one mistake or singling out one person. This is about everyone being held accountable to themselves, and each other. And that begins with me."

She continued, "And saying 'starting with me' is more relevant than you think. I've realized that along with everything we've been talking about, beginning with what matters most to our patients, as leader here, I'm responsible for bringing you all onboard."

Inquisitively, with a hint of skepticism, Zeller interrupted, "What do you mean by onboard?"

"Look, when I first started down this path with Jack, I looked at everything I did around here in the context of my job. I had no clue that I also had a larger role to play too. We all do."

"Okay, I'll bite," said Dr. Zeller.

Jane looked over at Jack, wondering if she was getting ahead of herself, and saw Jack's body language urging her on.

"Everything you do around here during the course of a day not only affects the patients, it affects everyone you work with. Of course our jobs are important, but we can have an even greater effect on things around here if we start thinking about what role we play too."

Dr. Zeller broke in, "What is this role you're talking about?"

"Look, we just described the four big values or attributes we were missing that morning, and for that matter, every day. Treating each other with respect, being a team player, really listening without judgment, creating a place where everyone, regardless of rank, feels safe to contribute..."

"Yes," said Ben, catching a glance from Mel, "the things we need to help us work well together."

"Exactly, Ben," said Jane. "Ethan's excellence as a surgeon, our ability to get things done around here, and the constant dedication all of you show up with every day aren't enough if we can't work as a team to solve our patients' problems. So Dr. Zeller, to answer your question, we all have the same role around here. Yes, we all need to show up with our talent and dedication, but without changing the way we approach working together, we're not going to change anything. We're here today because of Edie. She's not dead because we didn't know how to fix her; she died because we didn't know how to solve problems together. Because we had an OR full of talented people doing their own thing, not a team. Simply put, we need to learn to show up with more of a coaching mentality."

Jack took back the reins. "Now that you're all looking at 'how we show up here' a little differently, how do you think we're going to remember all of this and put it into practice?"

"It all comes back to the patients. We need to keep thinking about giving patients what they need. They need us to work more like a team," said Julie. Jane added, "Yes, the patients need to trust that we're all on the same page working as a team. If we want them to trust us, then they have to see us trusting each other. And there's no better way to illustrate that than by working in teams and talking to each other as coaches."

Zeller joined back in. "I get it, Jane. But talking about it here in a small group setting is one thing. Making your changes throughout Angels is a pipe dream. Your philosophy is interesting, but it's flawed. Even a small group of people will behave as they always have when things get really hot...unless you fit everyone with shock collars."

"That's why this meeting is only the beginning," explained Jack. "This will take time. It isn't a philosophy; it's a solution, a practice. And we've just done a little flyover. Ms. Carolli and I will be scheduling regular meetings to introduce tools that will help us on a daily basis. And yes, it's easier to get buy-in with a small group. But no matter how large the staff is here or anywhere else, they can all be broken down into small groups."

Letting that sink in, Jack ended the meeting feeling that they had plenty to think about, and any more talking would begin to dilute the message. As everyone walked out, with Lang first and fastest, Jack and Jane sat back and waited for the room to empty.

FIFTY-TWO

"What just happened, Jack? Ben confirmed himself as a tried and true ambassador and Zeller actually participated instead of following Lang's childish lead. I mean, he could have gone either way."

"It tells you a lot about what we're doing, Jane. You had once framed the Medical Executive Committee as Lang's cronies, a constant threat. And maybe we won't make believers out of all of them, but I think fewer of them will be trying to trip us up. As far as Lang goes, we had a physician just like him in Billings. He was younger but just as stubborn and self-centered. And coincidently, an excellent surgeon. He had no problem finding a job and left as quickly as he could. I wouldn't be surprised if Lang hastens his retirement rather than watch our changes come to fruition."

"Agreed. I've already been thinking about some incentives the board can come up with to help him out the door."

Jane sat for a moment, thinking to herself, when Jack asked, "Well, what's next?"

"Personally, Jack, I need to call Edie's husband Chris. A few weeks ago he called to ask if anything was going to change around here because of what happened. And I felt so hollow telling him that we're having meetings and working on checklists. Now I feel like, as horrible as it sounds, what happened to Edie is really going to jump-start something that's not only going to help it from happening again, but if we're successful, it will..." She didn't finish the sentence.

"What, Jane? Finish your thought."

"Well, I was about to say 'transform our entire culture,' but as I said before, that sounds so unreal. When I hear people use a term like that it sounds abstract and not at all doable."

"Well, answer me this, Jane. If you have a hospital with just over five thousand people running around with blinders on, doing their own thing, and then you turn it into a place with one thousand teams of five, solving problems together isn't that a cultural transformation?"

She smiled. "I guess it is."

"So where do we go from here, Jack?"

"Where do you want to go with all of this? You're the boss."

"I want to do what you all did in Montana. I want to bring this to the board and begin to develop a daily practice throughout Angels. It means starting at the top with one-to-ones, then small working groups, and then doing the same for the medical staff, and then... "

"Hold on a second, Jane. You're not going down the wrong path. But we started with just getting you onboard, and then worked our way into it with Ben and Melanie, and maybe we've ignited the spark in the rest of this small group today. But the board won't have the context needed to value what you're asking for. You're going to need to educate them first."

"Me?"

"You're the leader here. Making any significant change begins with you."

"I don't know where to start, Jack. I get it. I feel like I know it, but I just don't know where to start teaching it."

"Then break it down. Let's look at the main ideas you think they need to know."

Jane pulled out a sheet of paper and jotted down a few things.

"I know one thing for sure," she began. "I have to show them that designing a values-driven culture is not Kumbaya and holding hands. It has to be framed as substantive and measurable."

"Agreed."

"But where do I begin?"

Jack answered, "Begin with a valid supposition and figure out a way to put it into a measurable context they'll understand."

"C'mon Jack, I know you're trying to pull stuff out of me, but give me a little shove in the right direction, will you?"

"Okay. You have to keep it simple when introducing new concepts... maybe two or three new ideas max, no more. So what's the first concept you want to get across to them, Coach?"

Jane didn't even hesitate. "If we're going to start with a flyover, I'd have to start with the fact that everything we do must begin with what matters most to patients."

"Keep going," urged Jack.

"Then they'll have to start realizing the difference between our jobs and the parts we all play around here. How we all need to start interacting with each other as coaches."

"The part that they play too, Jane."

"Yes. And then I can show them the advantages of everyone working together in small teams."

"Jane, it all sounds good, but what about the measurable context aspect I mentioned?"

"I'll need to show them how our four behavioral values have a tangible direct application. Maybe we can use the HR example you and I talked about. For instance, if they think like I used to when it comes to evaluating and hiring staff around here, they depend on antiquated job description criteria that we both know doesn't include the most important behavioral values needed to get everyone aware of their coaching roles here and working in teams."

Jack said, "Sounds about right."

She kept going, "We need to create something like that real-life role description for them to grab onto. Something to complement the job description format we're using. Something that's consistently in place across every department, eventually."

"Great, Jane, they won't be able to argue with making everyone more accountable and cognizant of their coaching roles here. What else do they need to know up front?"

Jane referred to her list. "It really struck me today when the group said that if everyone in Edie's operating room had the 'role' knowledge we were talking about, it would have only taken one of them to change the course of that outcome. No one could argue with the fact that no one person is smarter than an entire group."

She continued, "Yes, Jack, I'd tell them that moving from individual to group problem solving is the best way...the only real way we can give our patients what they need."

"But you're going to have to tie it together by explaining how knowing about our roles along with our jobs is the prerequisite to that ever happening."

"I get it; we're on the same page, Jack."

"They're going to see this as a pretty tall order, Jane—when they ask you who's responsible for getting this done, what are you going to say?"

"It's up to me, isn't it, Jack? This is what leading is all about. If I want to do everything I'm tasked to do, beginning with improving patient care...it's all in my lap."

"But don't forget that the board is no different than the group today. You addressed the group today like a coach, not a CEO. You should treat the board the same way. Ideally, we're trying to get everyone to interact with each other as coaches, aren't we?"

"Absolutely. It's funny, Jack, but this began with building our relationship...with that contract or pact we agreed to. It's up to me to teach my staff how to make their one-on-one relationships work, and build from there."

"As long as you don't forget the glue that holds it all together."

"What do you mean?"

"Well, when you coach the board about building or designing relationships like this, what's the foundation, what'll keep everyone motivated and on the same page?"

Jane sat frozen for a moment. She knew he was talking about how to get everyone to better trust and respect each other so that they would work in teams...and then she blurted out, "Our patients want to trust that we're working together, and to give them what they need, we'll have to start showing up ready to trust and respect every member of our team."

Jack smiled. "We can do this. You're a good coach, Jane."

"I'm going to get us on the next board agenda, Jack."

"Not us, Jane. I'll work side by side with you building this out, but you don't need me at the board meeting. You'll be fine on your own."

EPILOGUE

THREE YEARS LATER

Dr. Norman Bell walked into Jane Carolli's office having never met the woman. But lately, it was pretty hard to work in the Seattle medical community without her name popping up. In his first year as CEO at New Seattle Hospital, Bell had read the ongoing press about Angels of Seattle, and Carolli in particular, but he really started paying attention to what she was doing after having lunch with Leslie Williston, the head of his HR department.

Leslie shared how New Seattle had seen a higher-than-normal staff attrition rate over the previous six months, and she couldn't put a finger on why. Nothing dramatic had changed personnel-wise, nor had they instituted any new policies or initiatives that might have caused a ruckus. As far as she knew, it was business as usual. And when she and Dr. Bell had lunch, Leslie felt compelled to share that during her exit interviews, a number of the departing staff mentioned they were trying to get hired at Angels. She told him, "When I asked them why, they said things like 'they listen to you over there' and 'everyone matters.'"

Norm knew most of the attrition they were experiencing was preventable. And when he was recently asked about employee satisfaction, he almost let out a maudlin chuckle, thinking the two words together were an oxymoron at New Seattle Hospital. His medical staff seemed less engaged and productive every day, and he had no idea how to fix any of it.

Shortly after the somewhat disturbing lunch he read another article, this time in *The Puget Sound Business Journal*, about Angels of Seattle's cultural transformation and how it affected their bottom line. Norm knew he had to talk to his counterpart, the woman behind the transformation. After all, she began her movement during the first year of her tenure, and here he was in his first year, barely keeping his head above water, his plate overflowing and no relief in sight.

———————————

When Jane Carolli received the request from Dr. Bell, asking to "pick her brain," she didn't hesitate. If there was one thing she had learned about the Patient-Driven Leadership practice they had developed, it was "share the wealth." And she wasn't alone. The pride she witnessed at Angels was palpable from top to bottom, and Jane's medical staff believed that every hospital around should be doing what they were doing. *The funny thing,* Jane thought, *is that a few years ago I couldn't imagine a physician coming to a nurse for advice, whether the nurse ran the hospital or not.* But Jane saw nurses and physicians teaming up every day, and everyone reaped the benefits... especially the patients.

"Well, Dr. Bell, what can we do for you today?"

"Well, ma'am..."

"Jane will do fine, Dr. Bell."

"Thank you, Jane, I'm not sure I know where to start. This is my first year running a hospital, and in all candor, I had no idea what I was getting into."

Jane smiled. "I hear you..."

"Norm." said Dr. Bell.

"I hear you, Norm. I came into this position a little over four years ago with a head full of leadership ideas and was stopped dead in my tracks, paralyzed by the never-ending managerial tasks that...well...never ended. And as far as staff cohesiveness, teamwork was practically nonexistent."

"Well, think déjà vu," said Norm. "Because that's exactly what I inherited."

Thinking back to the pre-Jack Martin days, Jane said, "Back then, before I brought Jack Martin onboard to kick-start everything, I spent less than 10 percent of my day actually leading, and the rest of the day managing fires... half of which should never have reached my desk."

"Jane, so you're saying a lot of the problems you had to solve just don't come up anymore?"

Jane paused and thought. "Not necessarily. We've come a long way here, but it's not a perfect world. That's just the nature of the beast. We're not perfect, but we're completely different and incredibly more cohesive."

Eager for anything to grasp onto, Norm asked, "Can you give me some specifics? Has it changed how you operate...pardon the pun."

Jane smiled. "What was once akin to herding five thousand or so cats, is now a cadre of small problem-solving teams that base their decision making on what matters most to patients. As a leader, Norm, think about having self-organized teams that pool their community intelligence to proactively solve a lot of problems instead of sending them up the ladder to your desk. It didn't happen overnight, but once the entire medical staff had agreed on a common organizational role, the issues that should never reach my desk in the first place...don't."

Norm thought out loud, "An entire staff of small teams..."

"We call them Patient-Centered Problem Solving Teams," Jane added. "And the beauty of it...we're all looking at every challenge that comes up through different lenses than we used to."

"What do you mean?"

"We're much more focused on finding the root cause of our problems and no longer satisfied with slapping a Band-Aid on a symptom, knowing it will eventually recur and become cyclic. Whenever possible, we all dig deep to find out where our challenges originate, and figure out solutions to hopefully get rid of them for good."

Norm asked, "And everyone bought into this approach—even your senior medical staff?"

"No, not everyone. But we knew when we started that we'd have some attrition. In fact, we lost one of our top surgeons; he opted for early retirement rather than change his ways."

"You're talking about Ethan Lang, aren't you?"

Jane started, "Well, I'd rather not..."

Norm interrupted, "It's okay, that was wrong of me to ask. As you know, this is a smaller medical community than one would think, and he's pretty well-known. May I ask, did 'this surgeon' just succumb and walk away?"

"Not quite, Norm, first he took a run at me by trying to initiate a no confidence vote, but it failed. But that's neither here nor there. The important thing is that some of his colleagues and the majority of my medical staff eventually came onboard. You have to start slowly. It started with me, then my team, and then we slowly moved through the medical staff." Jane paused for a few moments. "You see, Norm, nobody could argue about the concept of creating a patient-accountable culture."

Norm asked, "What do you mean exactly?"

"Well," said Jane, "one of the first things Jack Martin did when he came in as my new vice president for Medical Affairs was to help us all to realize that everything we do, every decision we make, must be determined by what matters most to patients."

"What's he up to now?"

Again Jane smiled, "Jack's still doing what he always does, coaching us to become better coaches ourselves. We work together pretty closely, always have. I think out of all of the things we've done, one I'm proudest of is our ability to showcase what nurses and doctors can do together as a true team."

Jane continued, "Jack will probably move on someday. He loves a challenge, and since this place has realized his goals, he'll probably look for another broken hospital to heal. It's funny, when he got here, he was chomping at the bit to bring what he'd done in a mid-sized Montana hospital to what he called 'The Big Leagues.' But I didn't learn until much further down the road that he wasn't sure it would work in such a large system. Seeing him...us...realize that success really meant a lot."

Norm was pleasantly overwhelmed. He knew he had a lot to learn. Without wanting to take more of Jane Carolli's time, he asked, "Jane, I know I'm just starting down this road...who else besides Jack Martin should I talk to as I do my initial due diligence?"

"Well, I'm sure if you ask, Jack will happily come your way to check what you have going on, and maybe even offer an initial diagnosis. If you have a few minutes while you're here, I suggest you also speak with two of our earliest adopters, Dr. Ben Waller, and our new director of Nursing, Melanie Swift Waller. They were both instrumental and would offer you some great insights."

"Sounds great."

"Oh, and one more thing," added Jane. "When Jack arrived, we first started talking about Patient-Driven Leadership and Patient-Accountable Cultures during a series of Never Event Investigations. We were dealing with a preventable death caused by our lack of communication and teamwork. I think you should talk to Chris Worden, the husband of the woman who died."

"He can't be a very big fan of yours, Jane."

"Not at first. He fought for and received a solid settlement, but he keeps coming back to the hospital intent on making sure that what happened to Edie won't happen to someone else. He was crazy in love with his wife. In fact, due to the settlement, the hospital started a patient safety committee, and Chris was asked to join, which he readily accepted. He told me that it gives him pleasure to think that he's helping to keep everyone accountable to their role, and he knows Edie would have wanted her death to mean something positive to others. You really ought to give him a call."

"I will. And thank you. I hope you can make time to do this again; I really want to learn more and figure out how to bring this program to New Seattle."

Jane said, "To that end, while you're here, let me see if I can get you a few minutes with Ben Waller and Melanie. Even if it's only for introductory purposes."

Norm walked down the hall in a slight daze, heading toward Melanie Swift Waller's office for a quick introduction. Again, he felt pleasantly overwhelmed, yet incredibly energized. The feeling in the corridors was palpably different than New Seattle. He couldn't put a finger on it and didn't know if it was a figment of his imagination, but things just felt so much calmer at Angels.

He was ushered into the office by the new director of Nursing's secretary to find both Wallers engaged in a conversation.

Melanie looked up, saying, "You must be Dr. Bell? Come on in and meet my husband, Dr. Ben Waller."

They exchanged pleasantries, sat down, and Ben said, "Well, Doctor, Jane tells us that you're interested in bringing Patient-Driven Leadership to New Seattle. That's pretty exciting."

"Exciting and intimidating," said Norm, "although I'm just in learning mode right now. I need to figure out if it will work there."

Melanie joined in, "It will work anywhere, and we're the proof of that. Although we didn't know it at the time, before Patient-Driven Leadership we were practically dysfunctional compared to now. If we could do it, anybody can."

"But it all starts with you, Dr. Bell," said Ben. "Your buy-in is critical—

then you'll get your board and management team to join you, then a few physicians and nurses...it's a process that requires baby steps...but believe me, you can do it."

"But Jane Carolli had Jack Martin," added Norm.

"Have you talked to Jack?" asked Mel.

"No, I've never met him."

"Well," continued Mel, "just go talk to him. I'll bet he'll be able to provide direction. Who knows, maybe Jane can figure out a way to loan him out to you periodically to get things going."

Ben added, "Good idea, Honey. Jack would probably like that. Things are going pretty well here, and I know Jack would jump at the chance of a new challenge."

"You know," said Mel, "although this process requires a commitment, it doesn't add to your workload, and to be honest, Dr. Bell, it's not rocket surgery. And although it really makes sense to most everyone, there will be some dissenters."

"Yes," said Ben, "but we lost a lot fewer people than I originally thought we would."

"What do you mean by lost?" asked Norm.

"I mean we were expecting some attrition—some people moving on. Especially the dinosaurs who weren't open to change...and we lost a few."

"And a few really surprised us," said Mel. "Dr. Zeller, the head of Anesthesiology was the physician on the original case that got the ball rolling. I thought for sure he would follow Dr. Lang's lead and retire early. But he bought in hook, line, and sinker. He now chairs the Medical Executive Committee and is one of Patient-Driven Leadership's biggest promoters."

"I guess I should talk to him too," said Norm. "We have a few dinosaurs too. Getting them onboard with anything is a challenge. I could tell you right now who would or wouldn't jump on the bandwagon."

"Don't be too sure, Doctor," said Ben. "I wouldn't be too quick to make assumptions. Yes, you should definitely talk with Dr. Zeller, and come back and talk with us anytime you want. But if you really want to get this thing going, sit down with Jack Martin."

Mel added, "And be ready to tell him what you think matters most to patients."

"What do you mean?" asked Norm.

Ben smiled. "We could tell you exactly what we mean, but that wouldn't be fair. Whether you call it connecting the dots or a light bulb moment, Jack Martin initially asked the right questions that led us to discover the answers. That's what coaches do. They ask you the right questions, listen without judgment, and guide you toward finding your own answers."

AFTERWORD

I have known Dr. Brian Wong for many years. He is a well-respected presence as a consultant, coach, and thought leader within the provider community. Even more meaningful to me is his devotion to the patient and his eagerness to place the patient at the center of the healthcare universe. That is why I feel honored to have been asked to preview *Heroes Need Not Apply*. What follows is my attempt to summarize what I believe to be some of the more important teachings that Brian has communicated in this engaging narrative.

Because the pace of change is progressing exponentially, organizational success going forward depends on the adaptability of its human capital. In *Heroes Need Not Apply*, Brian Wong illustrates an approach to the cultural transformation that is necessary to sustain healthcare organization (HCO) success. He advocates for creating team-based, patient-centric care, a clear departure from the hierarchical "Captain of the Ship" model that still dominates today's healthcare delivery "systems."

I appreciate Dr. Wong's points about waiting between stimulus and response and how reality is a result of not only changes in the environment but also how one chooses to respond to those changes.

Other points of relevance include:

1. Cultural change occurs one individual at a time, not by imposing an organization-wide initiative,
2. Attitude, not policy, is the foundation for acceptance. Individuals transform by connecting the dots in ways that allow them to align self-interest with the perceived benefits of changing,
3. Leaders coach through Socratic questioning, prompting individuals to understand their current assumptions and ask themselves whether

those assumptions remain valid in light of new insight, and

4. Focusing on the patient aligns caregivers' purpose by reconnecting them to the primary reason they chose to enter healthcare.

After thirty years of work at the HCO-physician interface, I have concluded that there are three essentials leading to success: *vision, dialogue,* and *measurement.* Without a great dream the default is self-interest. *Dialogue* is essential for building mutual understanding, mutual respect, and mutual trust, and for allowing creativity to emerge from the collective wisdom of the group. Unlike debate, which is like arm-wrestling where the most powerful wins, *dialogue* is self-organizing, non-linear, and the results are emergent and unpredictable. Essential to successful *dialogue* is a willingness to suspend judgment and to attentively listen to others. This is a realm into which heroes like Dr. Ethan Lang do not enter and in which the top-down behaviors of today's healthcare organizations perpetuate dysfunction. *Measurement* reflects attention and intention, two essential elements of self-fulfilling prophecy. *Measurement* directs and redirects action. You can't manage what you don't measure. More importantly, measuring tends to facilitate change in the direction intended. Dr. Wong and I have come to the same conclusions, and his story outlines the approach with elegant simplicity and clarity.

Don't be too skeptical of the behaviors portrayed at Angels of Seattle Hospital. They represent a composite of many hospitals, and I can assure you that in the course of my work I have on many occasions personally experienced each of the attitudinal/behavioral distortions that are described at Angels.

Dr. Ben Waller's progressive willingness to scale the "White Wall" and to speak out in support of the emerging new order reflects a journey that must be taken by the silent majority within the physician community.

In summary, everyone in the provider community would be well served by understanding and embracing Dr. Wong's approach to cultural transformation. It is culture and not policy that drives transformational change. On the journey to team-based and patient-centric care, the evolving healthcare system is indeed a place to which *heroes need not apply.*

Joseph S. Bujak, MD, FACP
Healthcare Speaker, Facilitator, and Consultant

APPENDIX

Following are three examples of the many tools we utilize to help organizations move closer to building a patient-accountable culture. Although we referenced these tools to guide the book's narrative and character development, these are actual coaching tools used by client organizations to improve patient safety daily.

THE PATIENT-DRIVEN LEADER T.R.U.S.T.E.D. CARD

All of us who work in hospitals relate to our organizations based on our job description. When working with our client organizations to develop a patient-accountable culture, our first step is to align every team member with a common role based on what matters most to patients. We all may have different jobs, but we all must have the same role. To consistently improve safety and quality and give patients what they need the most, we must first rally leaders, physicians, nurses, and staff around an organizational role description.

To help people stay accountable to their role, a number of our clients wear our T.R.U.S.T.E.D. cards daily to improve patient accountability. We continue to hear stories that showcase the need for a well-defined role description. From leaders, nurses, physicians, to HR departments, the cards are used daily in varying capacities: from defusing unsafe medical hierarchy conversations, to improving reward and recognition programs, and peer reviews.

T.R.U.S.T.E.D. CARD

Patient Accountable Culture Begins Here:

T	**TEAM PLAYER**	ROLE
R	**RESPONSIVE & RESPECTFUL**	
U	**UNDERSTANDING** *listens & learns without judgment*	
S	**SAFE** *easy to approach, invites my opinion*	
T	**TALENTED** *knowledgable, skilled & technically proficient*	JOB
E	**EXECUTES** *gets things done, gets results*	
D	**DEDICATED** *work ethic*	

"What matters most to patients determines how we practice as leaders."

THE
BEDSIDE
TRUST

© Bedside Trust

PATIENT-ACCOUNTABLE PACTS

Introduced in the book and road-tested in many organizations the Bedside Trust works with, this coaching tool for leaders engages everyone in a shared purpose and improves patient accountability at the one-to-one level. Client organizations use many variations of Patient-Accountable Pacts as coaching tools to reduce disruptive behavior, measure team problem-solving effectiveness, and improve team communications. The following pact is based on Jack Martin and Jane Carolli's commitment to each other.

PATIENT ACCOUNTABLE PACT FOR:

Jack Martin, MD, VPMA and Jane Carolli, RN, CEO

T.R.U.S.T.E.D. = Role Description Actions that matter most to our patients	The opposite of T.R.U.S.T.E.D. Actions that lead to unsafe and harmful events
Team player (makes others better)	Poor or lack of teamwork; "If you want it done right... do it yourself."
Responsive and respectful	Bad attitude; disrespectful; disdainful; sarcastic
Understanding, listening and learning w/o judgment	Rigid, intolerant; judgmental; impatient; cynical
Safe and inviting; approachable; preserves and protects confidentiality	Closed; shut down; threatening, unapproachable; intimidating; bullying, cursing, yelling
Talented: knowledge, proficiency, competency, judgment	Lacking in basic, necessary skills, competency, experience or judgment
Executes: gets results; gets things done; honors commitments	Unable to complete assignments, error-prone
Dedication: work ethic and timeliness	Poor attendance; high absenteeism/tardiness; lazy; leaves work for others

To encourage patient accountability and have a greater impact on improving care:

Jane promises to continue to stay in a learning mode and take the time to think before reacting. Jane will model and coach the T.R.U.S. actions that matter most to patients and be available to Jack when needed.

Jack promises to be a sounding board for Jane and continue to be a role model to improve teamwork. Jack will provide Jane undivided attention and offer continued trust and respect.

PERSONAL MISSION STATEMENT

While working with organizations to leverage the shared values of T.R.U.S.T.E.D., we assist leaders in developing a more relevant personal mission statement that informs their leadership practice. This self-accountability tool is generally thought of as a behavioral promise.

The following sample mission statement was developed by Jack Martin's character in the story. However, the actual content was derived from various mission statements developed by physicians and leaders we work with daily. I specifically included it to serve as a template and a starting point for creating your own.

JACK MARTIN'S PERSONAL MISSION STATEMENT

YOU may or may not be the CEO, but your leadership permeates all levels of the organization.

YOU are a leader who has the most impact on care not because you are better at your job, but because you help others see the role they can play to improve care.

YOU are respected by your peers not because you have all the answers, but because the questions you ask ensure patient-centered decisions.

YOUR conversations result in a perspective others value, and your actions make teamwork possible.

YOU are not interested in people following or being accountable to you, but insist everyone is accountable to the patient.

YOU know that a good team needs a good coach and that's what you are.

YOUR ability to connect and build trusting relationships throughout your team is a core competency that reaches each and every patient.

YOUR chief objective is to create change that benefits all patients.

YOU know that change is contingent on providing context, and for each problem you help solve, you play a central role in creating shared perspective that helps empower your team to act.

YOUR leadership practice is easy for your team to emulate because it's based on what matters most to patients.

YOU inquire, listen, and take the time to understand what challenges others, and offer clarity and set direction to discover each issue's root cause.

YOU are always open to alternative views, yet you guide decision making and influence others by putting what matters most to patients as the starting point of every solution.

YOU know that coaching your team to align their roles based on what matters most to patients is the only way to create a patient-accountable culture.

ABOUT THE AUTHOR

As a physician with a master's in public health from the University of California, Berkeley, Dr. Brian Wong's preoccupation with preventing disease, promoting health, and preserving quality of life through the organized efforts of teams, remains foundational today. Since his days as a resident in Family Medicine at Providence Medical Center (Seattle), he found himself in the same situation as every physician he's since met: overburdened with countless patient quality and safety initiatives, with no solution in sight. The "initiative overload" had distanced him and his colleagues from their patients.

During his years as a clinical practitioner, he kept seeking out solutions for what he saw as the biggest obstacle keeping physicians from giving patients the optimal care they needed and deserved. Over the ensuing two decades, during his chairmanship of Medical Quality at Providence and his medical directorships at Rainier Family Medical Group, Hospice of Seattle, The Good Health Plan of Washington, and Providence Clinic Network, Dr. Wong kept returning to the elemental question, "Where does improving patient care and the patient experience actually begin?"

He knew that all physicians work to improve patient care, but that wasn't enough. He searched for a way to ensure that all physicians and all health-care providers are always equipped to act in the best interest of their patients. His personal discovery of the true definition of patient-centered care came from the source itself, his patients. Dr. Wong has always looked to his patients to provide the clarity needed to make the right decisions. He realized early on that all staff members, regardless of their jobs, must work together based on what matters most to patients.

Dr. Wong developed his patient-centered theories into tangible solutions during his tenures as a healthcare partner and national director of Physician

Services at Arthur Andersen LLP, as president of Integrated Health Systems, and founding partner of Healthcare Performance Solutions.

In 2007, after years of clinical practice and applied research, Dr. Wong founded The Bedside Trust, a nationally recognized resource for healthcare systems across the country. Along with being a sought-after speaker and executive coach, he leads a faculty that works with medical staffs and executive teams to embed his "Patient-Driven Leadership" infrastructure in order to create patient-accountable cultures that result in improved safety and quality.

HEROES
NEED NOT
APPLY

How to Build a Patient-Accountable Culture Without Putting More on Your Plate

Brian D. Wong, MD, MPH

To learn more about Dr. Brian Wong's speaking and consulting services please visit:

www.HeroesNeedNotApply.com

If you would like to share your insights, ideas, or if you have questions for Dr. Brian Wong, you can e-mail him at:

Brian@HeroesNeedNotApply.com

This book is available in quantity discounts from Second River Healthcare.
Orders@SecondRiverHealthcare.com

Please visit:
www.SecondRiverHealthcare.com

For personal assistance please call:
(406) 586-8775

SECOND RIVER
HEALTHCARE